Y0-BXQ-897

Collected Poems

~

This book was published with the support of the Anonymous Fund for the Humanities of the University of Wisconsin–Madison.

Collected Poems

∿

With Notes toward the Memoirs

DJUNA BARNES

Selected and edited by

Phillip Herring and Osías Stutman

THE UNIVERSITY OF WISCONSIN PRESS

The University of Wisconsin Press
1930 Monroe Street
Madison, Wisconsin 53711

www.wisc.edu/wisconsinpress/

3 Henrietta Street
London WC2E 8LU, England

5   4   3   2   1

Printed in the United States of America

Library of Congress Cataloging-in-Publication Data
Barnes, Djuna.
[Poems]
Collected poems : with notes toward the memoirs /
selected and edited by Phillip Herring and Osías Stutman.
p. cm.
Includes bibliographical references (p.) and index.
ISBN 0-299-21230-0 (cloth : alk. paper) —
ISBN 0-299-21234-3 (pbk. : alk. paper)
1. Barnes, Djuna. 2. Novelists, American—20th century—Biography.
3. Lesbians—United States—Biography. I. Herring, Phillip F.
II. Stutman, Osías. III. Title.
PS3503.A614A6   2005
818'.5209—dc22   2005005462

Contents

Collected Poems

Notes toward the Memoirs

Acknowledgments

The editors are grateful for the assistance of Agustín Balbontín, Jackson R. Bryer, Donald Goertz, Richard Knowles, George T. McWhorter, Maurice Meisner, Alain and Jill Peyrot, Bill Ross, Charles Rossman, Jason Stieber, Howard Weinbrot, the University of Maryland Libraries, Houghton Library of Harvard University, the Archives Division of the Golda Meir Library at the University of Wisconsin–Milwaukee, and especially to Ruth Alvarez and Hank O'Neal. Our greatest debt is to the Special Collections, University of Maryland Libraries.

Editorial Comments

Osías Stutman has edited the poetry and the relevant notes for this volume and Phillip Herring has written the commentaries to the poems and edited the prose. Herring wrote the introduction, with borrowings from Stutman's epilogue to Djuna Barnes, *Poesía Reunida*. In the memoirs section, the spelling and punctuation of Djuna Barnes has been standardized, as she would have wished, and occasionally the syntax has been altered in the interest of clarity. In the poetry section, the few editorial changes have been noted. In no case has her meaning been altered intentionally.

GUIDE TO THE
Poems and Texts

Six acronyms are used in the notes: DB (Djuna Barnes), UMD (University of Maryland at College Park), HON (Hank O'Neal), "Envelope" (the copies of more than two hundred poems saved by HON), "List" (the list of forty-seven poems that DB prepared with HON during 1978–81), and *OED* (Oxford English Dictionary).

The DB collection at UMD: All the DB papers consulted for the present edition of the poems are in the Djuna Barnes Collection at UMD, housed in the Hornbake Library, where it occupies 102 linear feet. The collection includes published works, manuscripts, drafts, letters, drawings, and photographs, as well as DB's personal library from her apartment on Patchin Place. The material is kept in boxes, grouped as follows: Series I, personal papers (four boxes); II, correspondence; III, writings (thirteen boxes as well as map case 8 with several drawers for the oversize publications); IV and V, printed matter; VI, serial publications; VII, photographs; and VIII, artwork, drawings, illustrations to books, and paintings. The poetry folders are in boxes 8 through 11 in series III. The folders of the prose texts included in this volume are located in boxes 7 and 8.

The bulk of the collection was received between 1973 and 1977, with additions between 1980 and 1997. The first processing was done in March 1977 followed by fourteen other processings and revisions, the last being in July 1998. In the early version of the editors' notes, all the references to the UMD material used the July 1998 revision of the catalog (which was in the making at the time of the editors' visits to UMD in mid- and late 1998); however, for the present text they used the new reorganization done in May 2003 by Ruth M. Alvarez and Jason Stieber, which provides the box and a folder number (i.e., folder 8.9 *Approved Poems* means that it is the ninth folder located in box 8).

The texts used: The reader will note that the poems are arbitrarily divided into early (1911–29) and late (1938–82), leaving a lacuna; during this period there is no record of Barnes having written any poems. Of course, these were the years during which she wrote *Nightwood.* Most of the unpublished works are in the Late Poems section. For the location of the published work, the editors provide the actual reference, and for the early or late unpublished poems they give the title of the poem (or the first line), the name (in italics) of the UMD folder in which it is stored, and its box and folder number.

The editors have not altered the original published poems included in the Collected Poems, whether early or late, unless stated in the notes. In the un-published poems, they have tried to respect all the peculiarities of Barnes's style and punctuation, all the capitals, parentheses, quotation marks, hyphens, italics, underlined words, and words in other languages. In cases where Barnes made replacements without crossing out the words, the replacement word is inserted between braces { . . . }. The misspelled or mistyped words, when cor-rected by the editors, are indicated in the notes to the poem. This last aspect of the edition was not easy because of Barnes's use of correct but archaic words mingled with true misspellings. For example, "buriel" (fourth line of "Dereliction [When first I saw . . .]") seems a misspelling of "burial" but is correct Middle English (*OED*), while "burrough" for "burrow" in the seventh line of "Discontent" is a typing mistake.

"Notes toward the Memoirs" is quite a different case; in those documents there are a very large number of misspellings that have been silently corrected. Barnes seemed to use dictionaries, especially the *OED*, as her constant guide, but in the notes her memories flowed, and misspellings multiplied.

The texts and corrections: In the introduction the editors mention Barnes's style of writing and her practice of constant correction. Practically all the poems in the folders have some handwritten annotations or corrections. There are five types of corrections: (1) words crossed out and replaced by another word or words; (2) words that are not crossed out but have a word typed or handwritten above them; (3) complete lines interpolated in a poem, mostly handwritten and with lines or arrows indicating their place in the poem; (4) instructions (arrows, boxes) to change the place of a word, a line, or a stanza in a poem; (5) complex handwritten notes and commentaries, sometimes re-lated to a given word or line in a poem, sometimes apparently just marginal lines or notes that have nothing to do with the poem. This last type of mate-rial is extremely varied and includes possible corrections, lists of synonyms or homophonic words, notes about words that appear to be dictionary quo-tations, names of mythological characters from classic literature, and even totally unrelated materials (phone numbers, grocery lists, pharmacy lists, etc.). Most of the handwritten corrections are in ink (she rarely used pencil) that can be blue, black, red, green, and purple. Some pages were corrected with ink of several colors, and the editors suggested to Hank O'Neal that they might represent successive corrections. Unless stated specifically, all these poems have written in the upper right corner "Djuna Barnes, 5, Patchin Place, New York, N.Y. 10011" in three lines (occasionally she adds a fourth line, "U.S.A.").

The selection of poems: With respect to the actual selection of the poems, we may quote Marianne Moore in an epigraph to her own *Complete Poems* (London: Penguin Books, London, 1991, vii) that "omissions are not accidents" and reflect the balance between the preferences and prejudices of the editors. For the early or the late published poems, the order is chronological, except for "Rite of Spring," which appears after the quatrains of "Creatures in an Alphabet" because it is the logical link to the themes of the unpublished late poems that follow.

The eighteen previously unpublished poems of Barnes that the editors published in *Conjunctions* are as follows: "Portrait of a Lady Walking," "Lament for Wretches, Every One," "Discontent," "When the Kissing Flesh Is Gone," "Dereliction," "Dereliction (Augusta said . . .)," "Dereliction and Virgin Spring (Tell where is . . .)," "Satires (Man cannot purge . . .)," "Verse," "Laughing Lamentations of Dan Corbeau," "Laughing Lamentations (Lord, what is man . . .)," "The Bo Tree," "Discant (There should be gardens . . .)," "Discant (His mother said . . .)," "Discant (He said to the Don . . .)," "As Cried (And others ask . . .)," "As Cried (If gold falls sick . . .)," and "Therefore Sisters." All the poems appear in the Late Unpublished Poems section, except for "Portrait of a Lady Walking," which is in Early Unpublished Poems.

Early Poems Not Included in This Collection

PUBLISHED POEMS

After some deliberation the editors decided to include in the present volume all the published poems by DB known to them with the exception of an untitled poem (never published separately) in the article "How the Villagers Amuse Themselves" (*New York Morning Telegraph Sunday Magazine,* 26 November 1916; also in DB, *New York,* 247), two poems from *Ladies Almanack,* and the four verse chapters of *Ryder.*

UNPUBLISHED EARLY POEMS

The editors have excluded a few unpublished poems that either repeat material that seriously overlaps with included poems or else are undeveloped drafts. This seems a more defensible position than that of editorial preference and taste. The editors have consulted but not included the following early unpublished poems that in 1988 were in an *Early Poems* folder and now have folders of their own (the box and folder numbers appear in parentheses): "Love and the Bird" (9.23), "Hunting Song/Tally Ho" (9.15), "Exodus" (9.3), "Marine" (9.24), "Death and the Boy" (8.16), "Canterbury Summer for Chaucer" (11.1), "The Duel" (9.2), "The Fox" (9.10), and "Lament of Women" (9.18, different from the *Little Review* poem included in this collection). The folder 8.14 "Continuation of the poem of Michelangelo" is a typed copy of the last two stanzas of "Sonetto V" in the John Addington Symonds English translation with a two-line comment added by Barnes. Similarly, "Autumn" (8.13), "Finis" (9.9), "I'd have you think of me" (9.16), "Pastoral" (9.29), and "Saying Love" (10.17) filed in the old *Early Poems* folder were not included because they are versions, some of them with only a few changes or changes only in the title, of poems included in *A Book*.

The HON list and the "Envelope" of late unpublished poems: The HON list refers to the list of forty-seven poems prepared in 1978–81 by DB and HON and collected in a "working folder" (O'Neal, *"Life is painful,"* 92–95). In spite of the problems with this material, it has proven invaluable in determining the closest thing to a final version for many of the poems. These are clean typed copies with minor handwritten changes, and ten have the "OK" handwritten by DB. Some of them also have "German group" or "UK group" written by HON and relate to projects for a small book for a German editor and for Faber & Faber. Most of these clean copies were typed by HON. HON had an agreement with DB that he would write "Djuna Barnes, 5 Patchin Place, etc." as a single line at the top of the page to identify his copies, while the DB copies would have her usual three lines in the upper right corner (personal communication from HON). To reconstruct the list is difficult: following the transfer of the poems to UMD after DB's death, the fourteen attempts to catalog the collection (March 1977 to July 1988), and the recent fifteenth revision of May 2003, the contents of the "working folder" have been scattered in other folders. For example, 8.9 *Approved Poems* contains only six poems from the list. The 9.25 *Miscellaneous Completed Poems* has seven poems from the list, and 9.4 *Faber & Faber* has eight poems from the list. If one excludes the repeats between these three folders, however, they represent only seventeen poems from the list. After checking the more than two thousand pages of poetry in the remaining folders, the editors located forty-six of the forty-seven listed poems. Item no. 32 ("There should be gaboons for men to roll against audacity") seems to be a lost poem, since it is also missing in "Envelope."

What is "Envelope"? In September 1988 HON allowed Stutman to photocopy 202 pages of poetry (fifteen copies of poems published in magazines in

1911–71; 46 pages of early poems and 131 pages of poems written in Patchin Place, which contained the forty-six poems of the list plus ten others not included). HON related how the copies were made in autumn 1979 after water leaks from the upstairs apartment damaged DB's apartment. On that day DB was in the hospital, and on her return home, she found all the damage repaired and her flat newly painted (the water had not damaged her papers). HON made the copies and kept them, just in case such accidents recurred (O'Neal, *"Life is painful,"* 96–97). "Envelope" contains one to seven clean versions of forty-six of the forty-seven poems of the list (no. 32 is also missing here). However, six poems are repeats and only differ from each other in the first line or title, which reduces the list to forty poems, which is further reduced to thirty-six if one excludes the four late published poems ("The Walking-Mort," no. 7; "Rite of Spring," no. 19; "Galerie Religieuse," no. 27; and "Transfiguration" no. 28).

In spite of her bad eyesight and many infirmities, in 1978–81 DB made a serious effort to finish some poems and to select the best versions of others, intending to discard the rest (O'Neal, *"Life is painful,"* 59). HON remembers that sometimes he found DB burning papers in her chimney; these were especially recent copies that she felt were inadequate (*"Life is painful,"* 72). This fact may explain why the editors could not find in the UMD files various relatively clean copies of some poems in the "Envelope." On the other hand, we found nothing in the HON material that is not in UMD. In some cases (nos. 36 and 37), they were not the identical originals from which the HON copies were made, but rather versions clearly of the same text, except for some marginal handwritten notes. It is hard to tell whether some of these pages are misplaced among the many folders of DB's manuscripts or perhaps were never sent to UMD. However, it is clear that the copies that DB and HON worked on and copied during 1978–81 replace all the previous versions, regardless of dates (when dated). These versions were prototypes of both the eighteen poems that the editors published in *Conjunctions* and the late unpublished poems in the present collection. It should be kept in mind that the numbering of the poems was arbitrary and reflected more the order in which O'Neal wished to provide the poems to DB for work rather than a true thematic or chronological order (*"Life is painful,"* 92; and conversation, August 16, 1998).

Collected Poems

Introduction

Known mainly for *Nightwood* (1936), a tragic novel based on her life as an expatriate in Paris during the 1920s and a key text of literary modernism, Djuna Barnes (1892–1982) spent the last forty-two years of her reclusive life in a small Greenwich Village apartment mostly writing poems. This book constitutes the first publication of a "Collected Poems of Djuna Barnes," including all her early poetry (1911–29), all the late poems published during her lifetime (1938–82), and most of the completed poems that were in draft stage at the time of her death, including all the poems on a list of "approved" texts prepared by Barnes and Hank O'Neal during the years 1978–81.

Also published here are what the editors choose to call the "Notes toward the Memoirs," which, like the unpublished poems, are in diverse drafts written at various times and that at the time of her death bore at least four titles. Pages are missing, and narratives end abruptly, but most readers will be amused at her recollections of the expatriate scene in Paris during the 1920s. As drafts, these memoirs are understandably a bit repetitive, because the earlier texts went into the files to coexist with revisions, rather than into the trash bin. (The editors have removed repetitive material and noted the excisions.) Barnes's narratives here are often interrupted by notes for her play *The Antiphon* (1958), or various poem sequences, or deliciously wicked stories about writers who had the temerity to become more famous than she did. We learn what James Joyce wanted for his birthday, and what he was like to interview; we see every barb in Barnes's arsenal directed at Gertrude Stein, who refused to take her seriously as an aspiring writer, but once told her that she had pretty legs.[1] We find intimate revelations of T. S. Eliot, often prompted by the remarks of his new bride (and secretary) Valerie Fletcher. We see all of Paris fawning over Jean Cocteau, imitating his every gesture.

The received opinion that Djuna Barnes wrote practically nothing other than a few poems and a play during the last forty years of her life is about to change. This view is based simply on the number of her publications. The truth is that she worked hard during those years, even as she battled alcoholism and infirmity. When she died in 1982, her apartment was filled with notes, poetry, and memoirs that she had been working on in her last years. She told her brother Saxon that, after her death, he was to destroy all those notes and drafts, or, to be more precise, any written documents that he could not understand. Luckily for posterity, he sent them to the Djuna Barnes Collection at the University of Maryland, College Park, where they became part of a manuscript collection now occupying more than a hundred linear feet of publications, manuscripts, drafts, correspondence, drawings, and photographs. Although there is some correspondence elsewhere, principally at the University of Delaware, Maryland enjoys uncontested predominance as the main archive. Barnes sold her papers to that institution in 1972–73.[2]

With the exception of an untitled (and irrelevant) poem in "How the Villagers Amuse Themselves," two poems in *Ladies Almanack*, and four verse chapters of *Ryder*, all the published verse known to the editors has been included in this volume. The late production is fascinating because it shows the struggles of the mature poet with poems that are more in the draft stage than polished and complete. The editors try to bring some order to late drafts so that the reader can appreciate Barnes's poetic skill and see her literary efforts over the years as a continuing process.

Barnes published in all genres yet had a special commitment to poetry. Her first and last publications were poems, seventy-one years apart. To Hank O'Neal, her secretary in the last years of her life, she once said, "You will find it is better to write one good line than to make love all night," and here she was referring to poetry.[3] During her last years, she poured her passion into crafting these good lines and produced enough exciting poems to merit serious attention as an American poet. This became apparent when in 1998 the literary journal *Conjunctions* printed eighteen previously unpublished poems by Barnes, the best of her late years, revealing her successful new poetic experiments.[4] Prior to the *Conjunctions* publication, these poems had been unknown to all but a few scholars who had the patience to read through the many drafts.

In her ninety years of life, Djuna Barnes published sixty-eight poems: sixty-one between 1911 and 1929, and seven between 1938 and the year of her death, 1982; the latter are really only five poems since two are revisions of a poem published in 1938. To this, one can add *The Antiphon*, a play in Jacobean-Shakespearean free verse, and twenty-five quartets in the bestiary *Creatures in an Alphabet*, published in October 1982, four months after her death. Most of her poems were published in the literary supplements of newspapers and in literary journals. Some poems were published in books of her prose: eleven in *A Book* (1923), two in *Ladies Almanack* (1928); there are also the four book chapters of largely Chaucerian verse in her novel *Ryder* (1928). *A Book* was re-edited and republished in 1929 as *A Night Among the Horses* without any changes in the poems.[5] This collection includes eleven poems from *A Book* (which has not been reprinted since 1929), but not the poems from *Ladies Almanack* or *Ryder* since there have been recent reprints of both books and the poems are integral to their arguments. Finally, Barnes published only one book of poetry during her lifetime, *The Book of Repulsive Women* (1915), a pamphlet of eight poems that she cared so little for, she refused to authorize republication, which failed to stop a pirated edition in 1948.

The techniques of the early and the late poems are quite different: the early ones are mostly lyrical and transparently clear, while the later ones tend to be difficult experiments in modernism; but there is consistency in theme. Life is a dirty trick, death is fascinating, and loved ones will betray. One of Barnes's random notes states, "Man lives between the dreadful press of groin and grave," which seems to sum it up.[6] Also binding together early and late poems is the desire to shock the reader with horrifying images. Her friend Emily Coleman once wrote her, "You make horror beautiful—it is your greatest gift."[7] This particular gift can be seen fully displayed as early as *The Book of Repulsive Women.*

Although she could write love poems and evoke pastoral settings, Barnes's earlier poetry (1911–29) is often filled with a sense of the horror of modern life, and a common theme is death. Life is full of bitterness and betrayal; the future seems bleak, and morbid images predominate. The reasons are not hard to find if one looks at her early life. Her father, Wald Barnes, brought a mistress into the house to live with her family when Djuna Barnes was only five and had seven children with both her mother and the mistress over the years. When Wald's mother, Zadel, could no longer support the family with her journalism, Djuna Barnes's side of the family was exiled from the family farm in Huntington, Long Island, to survive as best it could in New York City. Occasionally in her poems one finds phrases that seem to express the bitterness of that earlier time: one note meant for Barnes's play *The Antiphon* has Miranda's mother say, "Go clean up the streets, go swab toilets in the park."

Wald Barnes believed in polygamy, and he even wrote a book extolling its virtues (later destroyed), but fearful of anti-polygamist wrath, he insisted on teaching the children at home. For lack of proper schooling, Djuna Barnes emerged from life on the farm with basically two survival skills, writing and drawing; the children learned a lot about the arts, but little about practical matters beyond the occasional farm work. Grandmother Zadel had connections in the publishing world; she also helped Djuna Barnes to develop her poetic sensibility, and it was always assumed that the girl would become a writer. After a few months of classes at the Art Students League of New York and Pratt Institute, Barnes landed a job as a reporter for the *Brooklyn Eagle*, where she was hired in large part because she could illustrate her articles. Eventually she worked for nearly every English-language newspaper in New York except the *New York Times*, which probably had higher standards for spelling, a subject that she never properly mastered.

Life in New York would be very hard for Barnes, and until she established her reputation as a journalist, she would pass many hungry days. Of course, since she had had it drilled into her since childhood that the only life was that of the artist, she spent her spare time writing poems in the hope that someday she would be noticed. Her writing activities were thus compartmentalized: journalism for survival, stories and poems for immortality.

By the time she was twenty-five or so, she had lived through more adversity than most people do in a lifetime. As a girl she had experienced some sort of sexual violation, probably incestuous in nature; her parents had divorced; her father had married her mother's chief rival, and Barnes had been thrust upon the world unprepared. Between 1915 and 1919, she lost her three great early loves: her principal tutor, grandmother Zadel, who died in 1917 of uterine cancer; Mary Pyne, who died in 1919 of tuberculosis; and Ernst (Putzi) Hanfstaengl, who rejected her to return to Munich after the First World War.[8] A line from one of her memoirs reveals her mood: "I have yet to be forgiven for having been abused." In one letter she wrote, "Melancholia, melancholia, it rides me like a bucking mare."[9]

Barnes was sent by *McCall's* magazine to Paris in 1921 to report on the expatriate scene. While in Paris, she had a tumultuous lesbian affair of eight years with Thelma Wood of Saint Louis, which became the subject of her most famous literary work, *Nightwood*, first published in 1936 in London by Faber & Faber, where her editor was T. S. Eliot. About two years later, Barnes showed her poems to Eliot, who didn't much care for them, telling her that she should stick to prose.

It is odd that Eliot was so wrong about Barnes the poet; certainly her potential was visible in 1938, for in his introduction to *Nightwood*, he had the foresight to suggest that the novel would appeal most strongly to readers of poetry. By this he may have meant that readers needed to pay close attention to the language and style of her prose. Until his death in 1965, T. S. Eliot served as an unpaid literary agent for Barnes, helping to edit her work and to negotiate translation rights. She was grateful for everything that Eliot did for her over the years, but her notes reveal her irritation with his severe judgment of her literary work. Barnes had such high standards that she may even have believed that his approval was necessary for her to feel that she had succeeded as a writer. Nobody else in her long life ever merited such esteem.

Though Eliot cared deeply for Barnes, he did not always esteem her writing. Against his better judgment, he recommended the publication of *The Antiphon* at Faber & Faber in London. In the last months of 1956, he wrote a blurb for Barnes's play that included the following statement: "It might be said of Miss Barnes, who is incontestably one of the original writers of our time, that never has so much genius been combined with so little talent."[10] Barnes was justifiably outraged and the blurb was suppressed, but such backhanded compliments are surely one reason for Barnes's frequent notes about his mean-spiritedness.

As Eliot helped Barnes edit her new play, she jotted several notes on conversations she had with him about the editorial process. In one note she complained of his "vague, self-deprecatory avuncularity and charm," saying that he was "really a rancorous testy man and unjust . . . {an} unkind old man with charm."[11] Another note on the same page says, "Tom did not brag of himself—he expected you to do it." What she hoped for was his praise, something more than his grudging remark that "she manages to justify herself."

What Eliot objected to was Barnes's preference for arcane vocabulary, gleaned from her reading in the *Oxford English Dictionary,* and a more general preference for obscurity and indirection. Perhaps he felt that if the poet of *The Waste Land* couldn't understand the play, even after editing it, the ordinary reader or playgoer would be quite lost. Though written in Jacobean-Shakespearean English, *The Antiphon* is set in the England of 1939. If one has a thorough knowledge of both Renaissance English and the life of Djuna Barnes, the play makes very good sense; however, the audience for such a work would be quite small.

Though Barnes had never gone to school for more than a few days, she became a very knowledgeable autodidact. Still, she probably had little sense of what an educated reading audience might be expected to know; because of her isolation, perhaps, she became so familiar with her elusive vocabulary and allusions that she came to assume that what she wrote would be generally understood. Or perhaps in her own mind, she wrote in these later years for a reader like T. S. Eliot, who had finished virtually all the requirements for a doctorate in philosophy at Harvard and who had won the Nobel Prize for literature. Barnes seemed to dismiss his objections to her obscurity, for *The Antiphon* and her late poetry rival in difficulty the work of any modernist writing in English.

Another famous writer is also prominent in Djuna Barnes's notes for pos-
terity: James Joyce. She did not know him quite as well as she did Eliot, but
she interviewed him a short time before *Ulysses* was published in 1922 and often
accompanied him to restaurants in the years that followed.[12] She thought
Joyce a bit distant and self-absorbed and liked to tell the story of his "hear-
ing somebody in the passing crowd say (not of course to him) 'There's mis-
fortune!' He hurriedly pulled out his saint's daybook (he always carried it) in
terror. 'It is an omen,' he said."[13]

Although Djuna Barnes's ideas for the memoirs were recycled into new
drafts with new titles, one does find innovative elements. For example, she
seemed greatly amused by a concert for four pianos given in Paris by George
Antheil (1900–59), who was hissed and booed as he sat at one piano waiting
for the other three pianists to appear on stage. As Barnes warmed to the task
of revision, in her next draft she made the scene even more preposterous:
"When George Antheil gave his opera for eight pianos and a fog horn, and the
riot that followed, one man putting up an umbrella over his head in the pit."[14]

She had similar fun exaggerating James Joyce's favorite drink, "a mixture
of anis-pernod-suze et fine—the strongest concoction known to man." Later
she increased the drink's octane level for even greater effect, describing it as
"a drink that would make any other person in the world completely idiotic
for a month."

To return to the subject of Barnes' poetry, a few words about her creative
process in the unpublished late poems should explain the editors' difficulty in
trying to bring order to chaos. Hank O'Neal describes in his diary what he
saw: "She does have a tendency to save everything that is on a piece of paper,
and to compound the problem she is forever making notations on anything
in sight, and it then must be saved for future reference. Poems on grocery
lists. All these papers are just piled up on her desk in no apparent order. She
said there are many good poems buried under the heaps and scraps, but a
mine-detector will be needed to find anything."[15]

Rather than continuing yesterday's draft, she would usually begin anew each
morning. She would first set down by hand the makings of a poem, type the
text, and then correct it time and again, thus producing multiple versions of
the same poem in a sequential order that is usually unclear. Typically she typed
an original with two carbon copies, and in almost every case the handwritten
corrections on the three versions are different. Then she would incorporate
some of the previous day's corrections, type a new version, and make new
corrections by hand. The exceptions are the clean versions in some folders of
poems called "finished," copied out by either Barnes or O'Neal.

She once wrote a friend, "I take far too much trouble with a verse, literally tens of pages to one stanza." Several years later she wrote another friend that, although the writing was going well, she would "change it, over and over, until the room [was] ten feet high with one canto." Consequently, Nancy Levine makes the appropriate remark, "Putting together the major poem cycle would be like reconstructing a living dinosaur from a huge pile of bone fragments."[16]

Poem sequences were begun and abandoned, with names such as "As Cried," "Gardens for Old Men," "Dereliction," "Nativity," "Obsequies," "Rakehell," "Sardonics," "Tom Fool," "Jackdaw," and "The Laughing Lamentations of Dan Corbeau." Except for a few salvaged poems, the harder she worked, the farther into obscurity the poems receded, until she took to creating a kind of salvage yard of parts that just might do in the right context. Unconnected ideas were compiled in lists, sometimes grocery lists, with lines between them, and often the more appealing ideas were then clipped into paper strips for use at a later time. The result was, of course, chaos.

The early poems of Djuna Barnes sometimes reveal her already to be working as a young poet in the gothic tradition, aptly termed "gothic modernism" (and described) by Deborah Tyler-Bennett, who is especially interested in late-nineteenth-century traditions of graveside poetry that Barnes's early style emulates.[17] (Of course, the Graveyard School was about a century earlier.) There one encounters images of undead women, beauty unmarred by the grave, beloved of grieving poets, who, writing haunting lines, formed a tradition of dedication to lost love. Barnes found in the gothic the reservoir of images and techniques she needed to commemorate her red-haired lover Mary Pyne, a famous Greenwich Village beauty and tuberculosis victim whom Barnes nursed in her final days in a sanatorium. The gothic tradition also appealed to her desire to shock readers with macabre images and reflected her youthful cynicism.

A wag might call Barnes the mortician of modernism or an anatomist of melancholy (Robert Burton's *Anatomy of Melancholy* was a favorite work), for her subject in the poems, early and late, is often death and what transpires before and after. However, the image of the mortician-poet performing an autopsy on the human condition would do injustice to Djuna Barnes's bawdy wit, for, among American writers of the twentieth century, her shocking sense of humor had few peers. How she could feel so depressed and be so witty at the same time is a key to her sensibility as a writer; sardonic wit is the dominant mood of the later poetry. Life was catastrophic and grimly humorous. As a result, Barnes suffered from depression and twice attempted suicide. The last time, she said that she swallowed all the pills in the twenty to thirty medicine bottles on her nightstand. Somehow, in gulping the medicine, she forgot the sleeping pills. Still, she immediately went to sleep and complained the next morning that she had never felt better in her life. And so she got up to begin another draft of some stage of an elusive poem.[18]

Often during her life, Barnes saw death as an escape from depression. Once in a hospital she was pronounced clinically dead and then revived; she was absolutely outraged to wake up alive and told anyone who would listen, "Now I have to do it all over again!" This combination of terrible despair and raucous humor, really her trademark, appears in various forms in the poems and memoirs.

The gothic remained part of her literary temperament early and late, though even in the early period, when it was most intense, not all her poems were in that tradition: one finds there bucolic and love poems mixed in. Still, the journey of Barnes the poet could be described as moving from the style of Aubrey Beardsley (1872–98) and *The Yellow Book* 1890s to the metaphysical poets with perhaps a turn in the direction of surrealism. In her early years in Greenwich Village, she was advertised by Guido Bruno as the American Beardsley, with ghoulish drawings a specialty; had she come earlier, she could have published in *The Yellow Book,* though she might have been charged with plagiarism.

In 1915 drawings of this sort were published in *The Book of Repulsive Women,* which contained poems that revealed depressing views of females in various states of decay. A poem in two stanzas called "Suicide" seems to take place in a morgue:

Corpse A:
>   They brought her in, a shattered small
> Cocoon,
> With a little bruisèd body
> Like a startled moon;
> And all the subtle symphonies of her
> A twilight rune.

Corpse B:
>   They gave her hurried shoves this way
> And that.
> Her body shock-abbreviated
> As a city cat.
> She lay out listlessly like some small mug
> Of beer gone flat.

A gentler poem on death from *A Book* is called "Finis":

> For you, for me? Why then the striking hour,
> The wind among the curtains, and the tread
> Of some late gardener pulling at the flower
> They'll lay between our hearts when we are dead.

Certainly other literary traditions come to mind when one contemplates Barnes's entire poetic career, the chief one being the metaphysical strain in poetry, visible in the later poems. Under the influence of John Donne (1572–1631) especially, the characteristic cynicism, humor, and gothic temperament of Barnes's early years combine to produce mature poetry that could hardly be mistaken for anyone else's. It is approximately two teaspoons of the metaphysical to one of anger and another of cynicism, a combination not found in the seventeenth-century poets she admired. In mood and difficulty her late poems are closer to her play *The Antiphon* than to any of her other works. Just as she chose Shakespearean-Jacobean English and the mood of Thomas Kyd's *Spanish Tragedy* for that play, being more at home in the earlier periods of English literature, she chose a metaphysical style for many of her late poems.

Perhaps Barnes became interested in the English metaphysical poets when she met T. S. Eliot in the middle 1930s, for he remained in contact with her and took an interest in her literary career. However, her interest could have developed earlier. In 1921 Eliot published the essays "The Metaphysical Poets" and "Andrew Marvell," later collecting them in *Selected Essays, 1919–1932,* a book that Barnes owned. His essay on the metaphysical poets was in fact a review of H. J. C. Grierson's *Metaphysical Lyrics and Poems of the Seventeenth Century* (1912), the book that most stimulated Eliot as well as other readers of the time to view this group of poets with more respect. She certainly knew about this Aberdeen professor, for in 1940 she was forced by her family's concern for her drinking to occupy a sanatorium room that Grierson had recently vacated, and she heard all the gossip about his alcoholic needs from the sanatorium staff.[19]

Although in his essay Eliot was right to wonder whether a term like *metaphysical* could encompass such an eclectic group of poets as that pulled together by Grierson, the term fits the poetry of the later Barnes. Eliot mentions a favored device, "the elaboration . . . of a figure of speech to the farthest stage to which ingenuity can carry it."[20] As an example of metaphysical conceit, he quotes the famous image of the lovers' grave from Donne's "Relique," "A bracelet of bright hair about the bone." As a modern example of metaphysical conceit, he could equally well have cited a simile from his own poem

"The Love Song of J. Alfred Prufrock" (1915), one comparing the evening to
"a patient etherized upon a table."

Barnes seems to have become familiar with Eliot's literary criticism and
poetry over the years, reading deeply in the metaphysical poets and Renais-
sance literature in general. This may be seen in the collection of books that
she sold to the University of Maryland (College Park), which supports her
often-stated opinion that the Renaissance was her favorite literary period. She
owned quite a number of Eliot volumes, various critical books, Donne's ser-
mons, his poems and prose, the poetry of George Herbert, two-volume sets
of Ben Jonson and Robert Herrick, and many other works of the period. She
owned a volume edited by Eliot's friend John Hayward, *Seventeenth Century Poetry:
An Anthology* (1948), and H. J. Massingham's *Treasury of Seventeenth Century English
Verse* (1931).[21]

Barnes noted the names Donne and Herrick on drafts of poems, and Hank
O'Neal mentions her admiration for Donne's poetry.[22] One product of this
admiration is her poem fragment "When the Kissing Flesh Is Gone," with a
nod to Donne's "Relique."

> When the kissing flesh is gone
> And tooth to tooth true lovers lie
> Idly snarling, bone to bone,
> Will you term that ecstasy?

Barnes shared with the metaphysical poets a delight in tricky meanings, diffi-
cult vocabulary. Obscurities such as *Bo Tree, skipjack, spawling, bombace,* and daugh-
ters of the *Gwash*—these terms send us to the *Oxford English Dictionary,* but unlike
many terms in James Joyce's *Finnegans Wake,* they can be found. Barnes's use of
such obscure words suggests her agreement with certain surrealist principles
as well, including resistance to everything that inhibits the free functioning of
the mind, a preference for dreamlike states, hallucinatory scenes that shock
without quite making sense. Consider her poem "Discant (There should be
gardens . . .)," a draft that never quite emerged from presurrealistic confusion:

> There should be gardens for old men
> To twitter in;
> Boscage too, for *Madames,* sports
> For memory, poor puff-balls of a day;
> Soundless virginals laid on to ply
> Suet to eat, and herbs to make them spin

Cuttle and costard on a plate, loud hay
To start the gnat—and then
Mulberry, to re-consider in—
Resign? repent?
Observe the *haute* meander of pavan
But never ask the one-foot snail
Which way you went.

But then consider "Lament for Wretches Every One," a poem that fulfills Barnes's wish to succeed at being at once very obscure and very powerful. Does one not sense here the spirit of surrealism alive and well?

As whales by dolphins slashed, bring on a school
Of lesser fins to passenger the blood,
So comes my general man, both my priest, and hood
To ask, "who drank baptism down in nothing flat?
Who cut the comb in half to see it quick
With buzzing backsides, quartered out of cells?
And sick
And staggered regents staling pedestals?"
I replied:
"What heard of Darkness oysters in your tide?"

In these late years Barnes could nevertheless produce perfectly lucid poems of considerable beauty, so it is clear that when she *was* obscure, she obviously meant to be. Here is "Discontent."

Truly, when I pause and stop to think
That with an hempen rope I'll spool to bed,
Aware that tears of mourners on the brink
Are merely spindrift of the shaken head,
Then, as the squirrel quarreling his nut,
I with my winter store am in dispute,
For none will burrow in to share my bread.

There is another interest in this poetry that merits careful consideration: religious themes. It may very well be the case that Barnes's religious poems owe much to her study of those of Eliot, Donne, and the metaphysical poets. However, the number of books on religion in her library constitutes a surprisingly large percentage of the total number. This is indeed puzzling. Hank O'Neal has written, "She said she was rarely, consciously religious, except the mysteries of life and death and what everything means, if life means anything at all."[23] She professed skepticism about religion as early as her poem "The Personal God" (1914), though at the same time she respected and at times envied the religious beliefs of others. Perhaps her views were somewhat conflicted, for her final will bequeathed the income from her copyrights in equal portion to the Author's League Fund and the Historical Churches Preservation Trust of London for the benefit of Saint Bride's Church of Fleet Street, an especially beautiful Christopher Wren church. (Eliot would certainly have approved.) On the other hand, she ferociously resisted the attempts of Emily Coleman to convert her to Catholicism.[24]

Since Barnes was not raised in a religious household and never joined a church, what is the source of her fascination with religion? One answer is simple, and another is more complex. For some eight years during the 1920s, she lived with Thelma Wood, who owned and read many books on religion and became a Catholic. Another answer could be that the historical and literary periods that most interested Barnes were ones in which religion was central to both the mind and the daily experience of the writers she admired. This would include Dante, the metaphysical poets (especially Donne, Herbert, Crashaw, and Vaughan), and T. S. Eliot. Eliot was at odds with virtually every important literary modernist on the subject of religion (one exception was H.D.), but Barnes shared his deep feeling for Dante, the Renaissance, the metaphysical poets, and all the beauty and intellectual intensity of those writers and traditions.

Still, many of the books that Barnes owned would not have helped her with the task of writing or understanding religious poetry. She admired the Catholic moral philosopher Josef Pieper (1904–97) and owned five volumes by him. So familiar was she with his work that, when grieving for her friend Dag Hammarskjöld, she could quote from Pieper: "I repeat again the words of that remarkable Catholic writer Josef Pieper . . . Hammarskjöld was a man who 'dared to walk straight up to fearfulness.'"[25] She used the line in a poem: "Viaticum (The victim and the victor . . .)."

Represented in her library were Aquinas's *On The Truth of the Catholic Faith: Summa Contra Gentiles*, four volumes by Martin Buber, a volume of Pentecostal hymns, a book called *Father Smith Instructs Jackson*, another called *When and How . . . The Anglican Church*. She owned Cardinal James Gibbons's *Faith of Our Fathers*, Karl Adam's *Spirit of Catholicism*, Rev. Alberts's *Validity of Anglican Orders*, five volumes by Jacques Maritain, two by Thomas Merton, and C. S. Lewis's

Screwtape Letters. Barnes owned one book that she would have known from reading T. S. Eliot—*The Devotions of Bishop [Lancelot] Andrewes.*

With this background in mind, readers will not be surprised to find that many of Barnes's later poems have religious themes. Readers fresh from reading *Nightwood* might well see the connection between the very noticeable theme of religion there and that of the poems. *Nightwood* ends with the Catholic convert Robin Vote seeking a religious experience in a small chapel. Barnes's poems have titles such as "First Communion," "Galerie Religieuse," "Fall-out over Heaven," "The Personal God," and "The Marian Year."

Barnes's first poem in this brilliant new style using biblical images was conceived in 1938 as "Transfiguration" and revised under the title "Fall-out over Heaven" to commemorate both Eliot's seventieth birthday (1958) and the arrival of the postatomic age. Here she envisions the dropping of the atom bomb and certain apocalyptic implications.

The atom, broken in the shell,
Licks up Eden's reach, and Hell.

To Adam back his rib is thrown;
A mole of woman quakes, undone.

From the ground the knife of Cain
Slays the brother it has slain.

To Moses' empty gorge, like smoke
Rush backward all the words he spoke.

Lucifer roars up from earth.
Down falls Christ into his death.

Another of her brilliant late religious poems went unpublished during her lifetime, the very obscure poem called "The Marian Year." It was probably inspired by early Italian Renaissance art.[26]

How should one mourn who never yet has been
In any trampled list at Umbria? Nor seen
The Unicorn thrust in his dousing beam?
And Mary from the manger of her gown,
Ride Jesus down.

Probably the most exciting poems that Djuna Barnes ever wrote are those of her last years, written in her flat in Patchin Place. They are sometimes called her poems of Patchin Place, and they are terra incognita for all but a very few readers. It is difficult to recognize disparate themes for the various cycles, with names like "As Cried," "Gardens for Old Men," "Derelictions," "Nativity," "Obsequies," "Rakehell," "Sardonics," "Tom Fool," "Jackdaw," and "The Laughing Lamentations of Dan Corbeau," because she often transferred lines from one cycle to another.

Not all the Patchin Place poems are dated, but those that are have dates between 1955 and 1981. Earlier poems are dated from the 1920s, and a few pages are from 1949 to 1951. Her technique, as always, was to write numerous versions of the same poem. For example, for the poem "Man cannot purge his body of its theme . . . ," there are hundreds of versions, and out of this multiplicity of drafts Barnes finally managed to distill a poem of only three lines called "Rite of Spring." At the University of Maryland there are six folders (296 pages) with varying versions of "Rite of Spring," some with more than twenty lines. The first poem in the first folder is a clean (and in this case final) version of three lines, dated 25 May 1980 with the following typewritten commentary: "Twenty years trying to finish this poem." This version of "Rite of Spring" appeared in *Grand Street* in 1982, three months before her death; the *New Yorker* had rejected it when William Shawn was editor.

Four years before Barnes died in 1982, Hank O'Neal, a producer of concerts and other musical events whose office was near her flat, received a request from their mutual friend the photographer Berenice Abbott (1898–1991) asking him to help Barnes cope with her many problems. Between September 1978 and May 1981, Barnes worked with his help, trying to bring order to the poems and to finish them. They sorted through the drafts and together set aside certain poems as "approved" for publication.[27] Among these was "Rite of Spring." He also helped with other matters, such as translations, the author's intellectual property rights, legal affairs, medical insurance, finances, taxes, and her visits to doctors. For about two years he spent many hours every week in her service, without pay, until she fired him, but not before he helped her set up thematic folders and a list of forty-seven poems considered on the approved list for publication. O'Neal's list was used as an editorial guide for this volume, which, however, is much more inclusive.

It might be well to include here an example of the sort of detective work that one might do with these little-examined poems. "To the Dead Favourite of Liu Ch'e" (1920), for example, is a beautiful poem in itself and interesting for historical reasons. Liu Ch'e (156–87 BC) became Wu-ti, the greatest of the Han emperors. In 1914 Ezra Pound had published his "Liu Ch'e" as an imagist poem and then included the poem in his volume *Lustra* (1916–17). First, let us examine his source, the translation in Herbert Allen Giles's *History of Chinese Literature:*

> The sound of rustling silk is stilled,
> With dust the marble courtyard filled;
> No footfalls echo on the floor,
> Fallen leaves in heaps block up the door . . .
> For she, my pride, my lovely one is lost
> And I am left, in hopeless anguish tossed.[28]

Now for Pound's imagist rendition of Giles's translation, clearly the better poem:

> The rustling of the silk is discontinued,
> Dust drifts over the courtyard,
> There is no sound of footfall, and the leaves
> Scurry into heaps and lie still,
> And she the rejoicer of the heart is beneath them:
> A wet leaf that clings to the threshold.[29]

Barnes's first stanza reads:

> The sound of rustling silk is stilled.
> With solemn dust the court is filled,
> No footfalls echo on the floor;
> A thousand leaves stop at her door,
> Her little golden drink is spilled.

Notice that in each poem the sequence of images is the same: silk, dust, footfalls, and leaves. Comparing the two, one might say that Barnes is rewriting Pound, but another look shows that Barnes has lifted two lines from Giles without so much as a footnote: "The sound of rustling silk is stilled," and "No footfalls echo on the floor." Pound has rewritten Giles, and Barnes has plagiarized Giles in the act of rewriting. Perhaps she knew the Pound poem at the time her poem was published, but she certainly used Giles's translation as her model. Another indication is that Giles gives no title, simply stating that the Liu Ch'e poem was "written upon the death of a harem favourite, to whom he was fondly attached."[30] Now notice Barnes's title: "To the Dead Favourite of Liu Ch'e," which gives the British spelling of "favorite."

"With solemn dust the court is filled" is no improvement on Giles, because dust cannot be solemn. "A thousand leaves stop at her door" is a deft touch that improves Giles's "Fallen leaves in heaps block up the door." But there the similarity ends, for Barnes went on to write three more stanzas skillfully piling up the images where Pound was content to be brief and suggestive, transforming a poem into one that Poe and Swinburne might have admired. We see the dead concubine's painted fan, the scattered tea, the crossed sleeves, the silent birds, and the fading cherry blossoms. It is as if her dead lover Mary Pyne had been discovered in Liu Ch'e's harem, though one cannot imagine a great Han emperor referring to his dead beloved's "black barbaric eyes." Barnes simply couldn't resist the Beardsleyesque touch.

Finally, it might be well to remind the reader that, when reading these poems, patience will be richly rewarded in the end. When the reader sees the fumbling nature of some of the drafts in this volume and wonders just what, finally, Barnes was attempting to accomplish by harvesting the most obscure words contained in the *Oxford English Dictionary*, that reader should look no further than "Therefore Sisters," one of the most powerful poems that Barnes wrote:

Therefore sisters now begin
With time-locked heel
To mourn the vanishing and mewing;
Taboo becomes obscene from too much wooing:
Glory rots, like any other green.

Therefore daughters of the Gwash
Look not for Orpheus the swan
Nor wash
The Traveller his boot
Both are gone.

Collected Poems

Early Published Poems
(1911–29)

The Dreamer

The night comes down, in ever-darkening shapes that
       seem—
To grope, with eerie fingers for the window—then—
To rest to sleep, enfolding me, as in a dream
       Faith—might I waken!

And drips the rain with seeming sad, insistent
       beat.
Shivering across the pane, drooping tear-wise,
And softly patters by, like little fearing feet.
       Faith—this weather!

The feathery ash is fluttered; there upon the
       pane,—
The dying fire casts a flickering ghostly beam,—
Then closes in the night and gently falling rain.
       Faith—what darkness!

Harper's Weekly, 24 June 1911, 11. First text published by DB when she was nineteen years old, signed "Djuna Chappell Barnes." The original is kept at UMD (map case 8, drawer 3, folder 19). There are copies in the HON folder (for details about this material, see page xviii).

    Commentary: In DB's very first publication, we find a nervous, edgy sleeper in what seems to be a spooky house on a stormy night. The night gropes with "eerie fingers," first for the window, then the dreamer, while "the dying fire casts a flickering ghostly beam." Clearly disturbed, this sleeper wishes to awaken but is not in so deep a slumber as not to notice the darkness and rain. Or perhaps the wish "Faith, might I awaken" is actually granted, so that the newly awakened sees the dying fire and gloomy room. In any case, whether the subject is asleep or awake, or, more likely, somewhere in between, the creepy atmosphere has found its counterpoint in our subject.

Call of the Night

Dark, and the wind-blurred pines,
     With a glimmer of light between.
Then I, entombed for an hourless night
     With the world of things unseen.

Mist, the dust of flowers,
     Leagues, heavy with promise of snow,
And a beckoning road 'twixt vale and hill,
     With the lure that all must know.

A light, my window's gleam,
     Soft, flaring its squares of red—
I loose the ache of the wilderness
     And long for the fire instead.

You too know, old fellow?
     Then, lift your head and bark.
It's just the call of the lonesome place,
     The winds and the housing dark.

Harper's Weekly, 23 December 1911, 12. Signed "Djuna Chappell Barnes," as are all of the 1914 poems on pp. 25–33.

Serenade

Three paces down the shore, low sounds the lute,
The better that my longing you may know;
I'm not asking you to come,
But—can't you go?

Three words, "I love you," and the whole is said—
The greatness of it throbs from sun to sun;
I'm not asking you to walk,
But—can't you run?

Three paces in the moonlight's glow I stand,
And here within the twilight beats my heart.
I'm not asking you to finish,
But—to start.

All-Story Cavalier Weekly, 16 May 1914, 228. Thanks to Bill Ross and George T. McWhorter.

When Emperors Are Out of Men!

These are things that must be done—
      Though they may not be nice—
When emperors are out of men
      And kittens out of mice.
We call the deed a righteous deed
      And murder, sacrifice!

No sacrificial laws are there
      To keep a man at play,
For this the maw within the maw
      Holds fast the reeking pay;
Small pay for that high episode—
      Our life from day to day.

There is no diary in war,
      No splendid paragraph,
Only that walled-in league of sound—
      The regimental laugh—
Only a too deep swig of pain
      That chokes us as we quaff!

And so they walk away in line
      Not knowing how nor when.
We will not know just when they die
      To speak the apt amen.
In death they will return to us
      To be bestowed again.

For that from out the ground we took
      In play of passion's ire,
Back to the earth we give it when
      Our sons lie down in fire.
Dear God, you sweat it out of us
      By the heat of your desire!

Upon hell's reddest butcher-block
     We lay the ready price,
For there are things that must be done
     Though they may not be nice,
When nations need their human prey
     And kittens need their mice!

All-Story Cavalier Weekly, 31 October 1914, 153. Thanks to Bill Ross and George T. McWhorter.

Just Lately Drummer Boy

His face is set with parapet
        Of tears that come too soon.
He has no drum, and so he plays
        Upon a pallid moon.
There is no music in his heart
        Yet he makes a little tune.

The soldiers walk, the soldiers stalk
        Like terrible gray wheat
And as they walk they make no sound,
        They move on phantom feet.
Incomplete their vestments are
        Their mission incomplete.

And so they pass, dim in the grass
        Outcome of shot and shell.
He has no music in his heart
        And yet he plays quite well.
Perhaps his music-master is
        Just lately—Israel.

The Trend, October 1914, 32.

Six Carried Her Away

They rode the car with spade,
With pickaxe and with blade,
To shape a grave, new made
    Wherein a girl must lie.

She gave the good of gain,
And suffered life's great pain
And in the hour of rain—
    Her call it came, to die.

She'd filled the barren street
With sound of wanton feet,
Advancing, till retreat
    Was asked of her, as pay.

And all who'd sought her out
In horror turned about,
For death is sick with doubt,
    Six carried her away.

Six men complete her fall;
Just six more feet, that's all;
Six feet of earth's good pall;
    For this they dig the wet.

She knew no future lease
On death's fine brand of peace
Could bring her mind's release
    Nor would her soul forget.

'Neath sky gone blank of stars
They fly the dancing cars,
And shoulder pick and bars,
    And hum a low refrain.

Bravely, here stretch her feet
Above that still, complete
Drab water winding sheet
       With border wet with rain.

Into the gaping park
Trailed round with lantern spark
They come, half hid by dark
       And half revealed by dawn.

They, from the rain-steeped town
From swinging boards drop down,
In grey of mist, and brown
       Of umber earth undone.

Of stalwart build and drape,
Till the mist reclaims their shape
With twist of foggy crepe,
       And all of them are—none.

The Trend, November 1914, 184.

Solitude

I seek no solitude but this—
      This one within my little room—
Four candles set apart to watch
      With wistful eyes the coming gloom.

And this, the shrouded mantelpiece
      And sober gap of fireside place;
And this, the darkened wonder of
      A framed picture of a face.

This is my perfect solitude
      Within my conquering abode,
The goal of haunting memories
      That walk beside a chartless road.

All-Story Cavalier Weekly, 28 November 1914, 152.

The Personal God

Creeds of a kind we've always had
To crouch by our dim fireside.
And here some gossiping wench arose
And the worth of some good name died;
Yea, the whole stale world went rocking
To the sting of her poisoned heels,
As a sky-car mangles the stars
For lack of the guiding wheels.
Though all of us sin most fully
When hushed in our neighbourly sweats,
Yet sometimes a man goes empty
For the urge of things, and forgets.
We stick to the same old pattern,
All daubed and kissed and marred,
But I'll use my own gray plaster
And I'll build me a personal God.
I'll breathe out his flaccid belly,
I'll cup out his sightless eyes,
I'll sob in the labor bending,
As I handle his plastic thighs.
And he shall be rash of judgment,
And slow in the use of the rod.
My God shall giggle in spite of himself,
In the way of a personal God.
He shall heed no other's message;
He shall follow no dusty path;
He'll believe in no written pity;
Nor yet in a written wrath;
He'll breed no circle of platters
Nor take root in your yearly fees;
He'll ask no patient toll of tears
Nor the terrible toll of the knees.
So, when all of you flock to your fancy,
The god that is always the same,
My God shall halt and be human
And his judgment shall halt and be lame.

Yea, the devil came down your pass,
Blown in on the strength of the breeze,
And because your Gods were duplicates
He shattered you on his knees.
I'll work my clay as I find it,
All hushed as it lies in the sod,
And he shall be built for better or worse
In the way of a Personal God.

The Trend, December 1914, 366.

Jungle Jargon

A monkey with a dreadful past
And sprawling bigotry of mind
Kept pinching all the cats behind
The scenery—it could not last.

It was a juggernaughty thing
Of jungles and of peasantry;
It laughed a little pleasantly,
It sang a song—it could not sing.

And down below where blind bears walk
Or lurch in tears upon a rug—
It is because they cannot hug,
It is because they cannot talk.

They are denied all things but weight
And rug value in days to come;
No wonder they are stricken dumb,
For this was never Dante's fate.

And, too, what lion has no wish
Napoleonlike to fold its hands
Upon its breast, to brew dread plans,
Or to receive a Judas kiss?

And in dim stalls, both huge and high,
Soft elephants still undulate
Like ole duennas out of date—
Like widows who may writhe and cry.

And out of corners soft with light
A thousand little puppy-wails—
They shake a thousand funny tails
Upon the other side of night.
A circus, if of pleasant kind,

Doth give the animals a chance
To note the foolishness of pants,
And so it brings content of mind.

"Djuna Barnes Probes the Souls of Jungle Folk at the Hippodrome Circus,"
New York Press, 14 February 1915. From Djuna Barnes, *New York,* 190.

Who Shall Atone?

I   How long upon our eyes this startled sweat
           Of steel?
      How long upon our souls must step
           The wanton heel?
      As the earth bursts up in wounds terrific
           As we kneel.

II   And must an age of speech be stifled in
           A moan?
      Must, too, the lead-shod lips of death slide
           On our own?
      And in some hour, not yet marked off in space
           Who shall atone?

III   Must all the ancient fabric of our life
           Lie rust?
      The simplest warp and woof of faith
           And earthly trust?
      The world but bitter hemp, heel-hetcheled
           In the dust?

IV   A million common lips that loved and kissed
           The Rod,
      Lips that moved upon the open books
           Of God
      Lie kissing little bubbling drops of blood
           Upon the sod.

V   And lilies are no longer what they were;
           Death gloats
      Upon those symphonies, swift stilled
           Within our throats.
      The battle front, the tragic lines despair
           The dead, their noles. [sic]

VI   Once flowers were flowers, and birds were birds,
                    Men were men;
            Now our Eastern blossoms do not bloom
                    Again;
            Our men but mounds of murder, and our birds
                    Quick carrion.

VII   O then is this the end of what we called
                    Accord?
            Is indeed the body of our trust
                    A tricky sword?
            And is this dreadful weight upon our hearts
                    Your knees, dear Lord.

New York Press Sunday Magazine, 4 April 1915, 1.

Harvest Time

Why couldn't we have known
When love was sweet,
When the world and I lay dreaming
At your feet,
That all the barren things would blossom
In the wheat?

Why couldn't we have known
No bitter gloom
Or any troubled sense or knowledge
Of the tomb.
Could be a master-work when poppies lean,
Bleeding into bloom?

Why couldn't we have known
In younger years—
When life and love were lived
Undimmed by tears—
That no cry of youth or age is wider
Than the ears?

All-Story Cavalier Weekly, 22 May 1915, 369.

The Master—Dead

His sighs were sonnets out of school.
He made replies
Like any wise artistic fool
With gabled eyes
He told his truths as men have done
Since men knew lies.

He was alone, the master grain
In all the crowd.
A thousand hammers on his heart
Beat high and loud
Aye, it's a wasted field indeed,
Untilled, unplowed.

His sense of tolerance was marred
By inborn leers.
His eyes, the fountain springs of life,
Half warped with tears.
Some said that he had wept too much
Throughout the years.

And so he gambled at life's board
(Breath has its price)
A prison's built with iron bars,
A man with dice
A kitten is king because
It knows its mice.

And so he died, yet lying dead
Was incomplete;
For though his head laughed loud in hell,
The shudd'ring wheat
In god's stern granaries was stirred
By his great feet.

Though half of him, irreverence,
And half retrieves,
His chest he left beneath our sod
And leaves;
And in the dawn, when God is still—
It heaves.

All-Story Cavalier Weekly, 5 June 1915, 768.

Tramp Summer

He heard the spinning blond cocoon
Embroidering an early moon,
Until it broke its thread too soon
And died.

A sparrow with frail, sprawling feet
Sang to a summer over sweet,
And lolled a little in the heat,
And sighed.

And all the daisies, coarse yet kind,
Much like a Titan woman's mind,
Leaned belling into the wind,
Or drooped to hush.

With lips blown tragic in the air
A man lay flat upturned to stare
As though he had been painted there
By some vast brush.

All-Story Cavalier Weekly, 26 June 1915, 454.

This Much and More

If my lover were a comet
　　　　Hung in air,
I would braid my leaping body
　　　　In his hair.

Yea, if they buried him ten leagues
　　　　Beneath the loam,
My fingers they would learn to dig
　　　　And I'd plunge home!

All-Story Cavalier Weekly, 4 September 1915, 81.

The Book of Repulsive Women

Both the first edition (*The Book of Repulsive Women, 8 Rhythms and 5 Drawings, Bruno Chap Books* 2, no. 6 [November 1915]: 91–92, 93, 94, 95, 96, 97, 98, 99) located in box 12, folder 10 at UMD and the 1994 edition (Los Angeles: Sun & Moon Press, 1994, 13–15, 17, 19–21, 23–24, 25, 27–29, 31–33, 35) were consulted. The 1989 edition by Sun & Moon Press (20 pages, Los Angeles, no page numbers) is defective, and four lines from "To a Cabaret Dancer" are missing (the last two lines from the seventh and the first two of the eighth stanzas).

Commentary: Andrew Field was right about *The Book of Repulsive Women;* Guido Bruno could have been hauled before the court for publishing these eight poems and five drawings, and DB could have accompanied him as the author. The notoriety allowed Bruno to raise the price of this pamphlet from fifteen cents to fifty, more than triple the original price, but it is a safe bet that DB never shared in the additional profit (see Field, *Djuna,* 67, for details of the publication and reception of *The Book of Repulsive Women.*). She didn't like the poems and never wished them reprinted, but they have enjoyed a reputation in certain quarters, and some think them celebratory of lesbian life. Whatever one's view of them and their morbidity or the general sense of depression, they do represent quite a leap in both skill and imagination from "The Dreamer."

From Fifth Avenue Up

Someday beneath some hard
      Capricious star—
Spreading its light a little
Over far.
We'll know you for the woman
That you are.

For though one took you, hurled you
Out of space,
With your legs half strangled
In your lace.
You'd lip the world to madness
On your face.

We'd see your body in the grass
With cool pale eyes.
We'd strain to touch those lang'rous
Length of thighs:
And hear your short sharp modern
Babylonic cries.

It wouldn't go. We'd feel you
Coil in fear
Leaning across the fertile
Fields to leer
As you urged some bitter secret
Through the ear.

We see your arms grow humid
In the heat;
We see your damp chemise lie
Pulsing in the beat
Of the over-hearts left oozing
At your feet.

See you sagging down with bulging
Hair to sip,
The dappled damp from some vague
Under lip.
Your soft saliva, loosed
With orgy, drip.

Once we'd not have called this
Woman you—
When leaning above your mother's
Spleen you drew
Your mouth across her breast as
Trick musicians do.

Plunging grandly out to fall
Upon your face.
Naked-female-baby
In grimace.
With your belly bulging stately
Into space.

In General

What altar cloth, what rag of worth
Unpriced?
What turn of card, what trick of game
Undiced?
And you we valued still a little
More than Christ.

From Third Avenue On

And now she walks on out turned feet
      Beside the litter in the street
Or rolls beneath a dirty sheet
      Within the town.
She does not stir to doff her dress,
She does not kneel low to confess,
A little conscience, no distress
      And settles down.

Ah God! she settles down we say;
It means her powers slip away
It means she draws back day by day
      From good or bad.

And so she looks upon the floor
Or listens at an open door
Or lies her down, upturned to snore
      Both loud and sad.

Or sits beside the chinaware,
Sits mouthing meekly in a chair,
With over-curled, hard waving hair
      Above her eyes.
Or grins too vacant into space—
A vacant space is in her face—
Where nothing came to take the place
      Of high hard cries.

Or yet we hear her on the stairs
With some few elements of prayers,
Until she breaks it off and swears
      A loved bad word.
Somewhere beneath her hurried curse,
A corpse lies bounding in a hearse;
And friends and relatives disperse,
      And are not stirred.

Those living dead up in their rooms
Must note how partial are the tombs,
That take men back into their wombs
      While theirs must fast.
And those who have their blooms in jars

No longer stare into the stars,
Instead, they watch the dinky cars—
      And live aghast.

Seen from the "L"

So she stands—nude—stretching dully
Two amber combs loll through her hair
A vague molested carpet pitches
Down the dusty length of stair.
She does not see, she does not care
                    It's always there.

The frail mosaic on her window
Facing starkly toward the street
Is scribbled there by tipsy sparrows—
Etched there with their rocking feet.
Is fashioned too, by every beat
                    Of shirt and sheet.

Still her clothing is less risky
Than her body in its prime.
They are chain-stitched and so is she
Chain-stitched to her soul for time.
Raveling grandly into vice
Dropping crooked into rhyme.
Slipping through the stitch of virtue,
                    Into crime.

Though her lips are vague as fancy
In her youth—
They bloom vivid and repulsive
As the truth.
Even vases in the making
                    Are uncouth.

In Particular

What loin-cloth, what rag of wrong
Unpriced?
What turn of body, what of lust
Undiced?
So we've worshipped you a little
More than Christ.

Twilight of the Illicit

You, with your long blank udders
And your calms,
Your spotted linen and your
Slack'ning arms.
With satiated fingers dragging
at your palms.

Your knees set far apart like
Heavy spheres;
With discs upon your eyes like
Husks of tears;
And great ghastly loops of gold
Snared in your ears.

Your dying hair hand-beaten
'Round your head.
Lips, long lengthened by wise words
Unsaid.
And in your living all grimaces
Of the dead.

One sees you sitting in the sun
Asleep;
With the sweeter gifts you had
And didn't keep,
One grieves that the altars of
Your vice lie deep.

You, the twilight powder of
A fire-wet dawn;
You, the massive mother of
Illicit spawn;
While the others shrink in virtue
You have borne.

We'll see you staring in the sun
A few more years,
With discs upon your eyes like
Husks of tears;
And great ghastly loops of gold
Snared in your ears.

To a Cabaret Dancer

A thousand lights had smitten her
      Into this thing;
Life had taken her and given her
      One place to sing.

She came with laughter wide and calm;
      And splendid grace;
And looked between the lights and wine
      For one fine face.

And found life only passion wide
      'Twixt mouth and wine.
She ceased to search, and growing wise
      Became less fine.

Yet some wondrous thing within the mess
      Was held in check—
Was missing as she groped and clung
      About his neck.

One master chord we couldn't sound
      For lost the keys,
Yet she hinted of it as she sang
      Between our knees.

We watched her come with subtle fire
      And learned feet,
Stumbling among the lustful drunk
      Yet somehow sweet.

We saw the crimson leave her cheeks
      Flame in her eyes;
For when a woman lives in awful haste
      A woman dies.

The jests that lit our hours by night
        And made them gay,
Soiled a sweet and ignorant soul
        And fouled its play.

Barriers and heart both broken—dust
        Beneath her feet.
You've passed her forty times and sneered
        Out in the street.

A thousand jibes had driven her
        To this at last;
Till the ruined crimson of her lips
        Grew vague and vast.

Until her songless soul admits
        Time comes to kill:
You pay her price and wonder why
        You need her still.

Suicide

Corpse A

                  They brought her in, a shattered small
          Cocoon,
          With a little bruisèd body like
          A startled moon;
          And all the subtle symphonies of her
          A twilight rune.

Corpse B

                  They gave her hurried shoves this way
          And that.
          Her body shock-abbreviated
          As a city cat.
          She lay out listlessly like some small mug
          Of beer gone flat.

Death

Down the dusty highway, on the broken road,
      With curls as thin as smoke is hovering round his head,
Came the slow procession with its dreaming load:
      The man who stopped his living that he might be dead.

On the sodden plank-bridge, musing though the town,
      Thus, with hands before him, crossed like girls who pray,
So the vivid corpse came, with his head bent down,
      In the chill of morning and through the common day.

Straight his lips, *sans* laughter, all the pain left in,
      Quiet as a chancel that breathes a morning prayer;
So the stately body, with its rigid chin
      And its startled, leaping-high, thin, damp curls of hair.

Thus does one consider, death and man debate,
      Some must leave to-morrow, but some must know to-day,
And some approach too early, but most approach too late,
      When the tang of random youth has dropped into decay.

Heavy feet, like women's hands pregnant with vast prayer,
All his muted splendor caught upon Death's loom,
With his throat fast fettered to the branches of his hair,
But with soul tobogganing upon the sled of doom.

Through the dark'ning city to a narrow space,
      With a song between his teeth, silence in control,
With a little humor clenched within his face
      And a little wonder wedged within his soul.

All-Story Cavalier Weekly, 4 March 1916, 406. DB wrote "awful" in the margin of the original copy ca. 1978. In "Envelope."

In Conclusion

Not every pipe is builded for our lays
       Some hour the echo of our feet will flee,
       For, all unenvied, high eternity
Is deep with those who leave eternal ways.

No hate, no love, and no parental prayer
       Lives in the young; old wines they do not hold,
       And hate and love are outlived by the old—
Too near to death for passion and despair.

And we who live our time always too fast,
       Whose lips beneath the kiss fall into dust
       Will feel {up} on the blade of Time untimely rust,
So all of us outlive our hearts at last.

Yet I who loved, and you who loves and all
       Who rose more steeply and were not above
       Great human pity and {most} inhuman love,
Will not be found ignoble when we fall.

All-Story Cavalier Weekly, 6 May 1916, 764. The changes in lines 11 and 15 were handwritten in the margins of the original ca. 1978. In "Envelope."

Dust

The Nation falls.   And still the Hosts arise
        To walk above this hemisphere of pain,
Built by the voice of man.   Indebted to those eyes
        That bled the mind's deep blood of old surprise
That nothing lives, and nothing ever dies.

~

As once, this road we walk each hour above
        Was every hour prostrate before the Lord,
The levelled prayer of some too human flame,
        An Idol dropped to dust while still adored.

And so it is for every temple praised
        Some whispered penance to the dust is flung
And there to cleave, until some woe shall stir
        The cloistered ashes of that anguished tongue.

And I, who in mine own grave am a guest,
        Am a stranger in myself as absolute.
        I banquet at myself in high dispute
And to myself pledge wines still unaddressed.

So all who have been flung up from the Pangs,
        And by some Hand retossed before the fruit
Will once again be found beneath that flower
        Within the clenched fingers of its root.

And I—I, too, am falling to that height
        Once with the Kneeling, emptied of their breath
For you who walk above, to call it Dust,
        For us below, the Miracle of Death.

All-Story Cavalier Weekly, 3 June 1916, 642.

Birth

Fore-loved, fore-crowned, and fore-betrayed,
     And thrice our quality been weighed,
  And thrice our hearts been spit with steel
  To prove us worthier to feel
Both love and hate creep through that blade,
     The wings of doom press tip to tip,
And all dead hands like bricks are laid
  And reach like mansions to the sky—
     The parting, weeping lip to lip,
  That all things born must always die.
And that the seed of Nothing lies
  Yet here within this envied Much—
  So we are forecast, and of such
The child's first sobbing prophesies.

All-Story Cavalier Weekly 24 June 1916, 442. HON contains a copy with "awful" handwritten by DB.

The Yellow Jar

White butterflies are creeping near
    This yellow jar where rose-leaves lie,
Like simple nuns in gowns of fear,
    Like humor and like tragedy.

And down they steal with throbbing wing
    Across the pool of shadows, where
The other bowl of dust is king
    With blossoms past, with tear, with prayer.

One was the rose you brought, and one
    Was you. The symbol lied—it seemed
You were the summit of the sun;
    Now you are less than you dreamed.

In life we loved you, and in death
    There is devotion for you, too;
Only the witless human breath
    Is mourning for the death in you.

Yet what of you, I wonder, stands
    Without the stillness of the room,
Beyond the reach of rising hands,
    Still smiling at this china tomb!

While butterflies are creeping past
    The jar of death, the yellow jar;
For butterflies are not the last
    To sense things are not as they are!

Munsey's Magazine, September 1916, 605.

A Last Toast

My tears are falling one by one
Upon the silence of this bed;
Like rain they crown his quiet head
Like moons they slip within his hair;
They came like wine and passed like prayer
Into the goblets of the dead.

All-Story Cavalier Weekly, 9 September 1916, 379.

To an Idol

It sat with folded hands and grinned
      Upon our sky.
Each ochre lock that streaked its head
      Was curled and dry.
A little dust of aged despair
      Was in each eye.

Both somber wooden breasts seemed weighed
      With heavy tears,
Dropped and forgotten long ago
      In other years,
But waiting still to fall like fate
      Upon the ears.

Beneath its girdle and its chains
      Each carved foot stood;
Incapable of pangs or pains,
      Or sweats of blood.
Conceived in superstition
      And doomed in wood.

And yet behind abysmal leer
      And faulty frown,
Throbbing faintly out of space
      That shadows drown,
We hear God's grim machinery
      Run down.

All-Story Cavalier Weekly, 16 September 1916, 480.

Shadows

A little trellis stood beside my head,
And all the tiny fruitage of its vine
Fashioned a shadowy cover to my bed,
And I was madly drunk on shadow wine!

A lily bell hung sidewise, leaning down,
And gowned me in a robe so light and long;
And so I dreamed, and drank, and slept, and heard
The lily's song.

Lo, for a house, the shadow of the moon;
For golden money, all the daisy rings;
And for my love, the meadow at my side—
Thus tramps are kings!

Munsey's Magazine, November 1916, 272.

Love Song

I am the woman—it is I—
Through all my pain I suffer peace;
Through all my peace I suffer pain;
This insufficient agony—
This stress of woe I cannot feel—
These knees that cannot bend to kneel—
A corpse that flames and cannot die—
A candle with the wick torn through—
These are the things from which I grew
Into the woman whom you hate—
She whom you loved before you knew—
Loved, loved so much before you knew.

All I cannot weep—in tears,
All I cannot pray—in prayers,
For it is so the wild world moves,
And it is so that Tame Man loves.
It is for this books fall to ruin;
For this great houses mold and fall;
For this the infant gown, the pall;
For this the veil that eyes weep through,
For this the birds go stumbling down
Into the cycled ages where
Their squandered plumage rends the air.
For this each living thing that dies
Shakes loose a soul that will arise
Like ivory against black space—
A quiet thing, but with a face
Wherein a weeping mouth is built—
A little wound where grief is spilt.

I am the woman—even so—
Through the years I have not swerved,
Through the years I've altered not.
What changes have I yet to know?
Through what gardens must I crawl?

How many roses yet must fall?
How many flowers yet must blow?
How many blossoms yet must rot?

How many thorns must I yet bear
Within the clenched fists of despair?
To be again she whom you loved—
Loved you so much, so much did care—
Loved, loved so much, so much did care!

All-Story Cavalier Weekly, 18 November 1916, 744.

Lines to a Lady

Lay her under the rusty grass,
     With her two eyes heavy and blind and done;
Her two hands crossed beneath her breast
     One on one.

Lay her out in the paling eve,
     With its sudden tears and white birch trees;
And let her passing seem to be
     One with ease.

Close her out of this hour of grief,
     And casting the earth on her, like a breath,
Sew her tenderly, that she may
     Reap her death!

And close her eyes, close her lips,
     For still, too still is her smitten tongue;
Her hour's over, her breath has passed,
     And her song is sung.

Lay her under the wild red grass
     In the fields death-tossed and bowed with rain;
And let her silence seem to move
     Within the grain.

All-Story Cavalier Weekly, 1 June 1918, 764. In box 12, folder 37. Copies in 9.25, *Miscellaneous Completed Poems* at UMD. Included in Braithwaite, *Anthology of Magazine Verse*.

The Lament of Women

The Little Review 5, no. 8 (December 1918): 37–38. DB's story *A Night Among the Horses* appears in the same issue (3–10). *LR* eventually published seven more stories by DB.

Commentary: In the second poem, "To ——," the speaker is troubled by a simultaneous attachment to two lovers made miserable by the poet persona's apparent infidelity, but the voice pleads that hers is a "virgin's gaze" nonetheless. The man she sleeps with feels "half wounded"; perhaps he is Courtenay Lemon, a writer with whom she lived in Greenwich Village between 1917 and 1919. But she has greater cause to feel wounded, "For I have words to every man's distress / And some forgotten ailing hand in hell / First tore this dress." Clearly this refers to a violent act that took her virginity. Her present lover should understand the nature of her commitment to him and an unnamed other: at death his dust will know a thousand years of peace, while hers will mix with another's in the grave's restless union.

Ah My God!

Ah my God, what is it that we love!
This flesh laid on us like a wrinkled glove?
Bones caught in haste from out some lustful bed,
And for momentum, this a devil's shove.

What is it that hurriedly we kiss,
This mouth that seeks our own, or still more this
Small sorry eye within the cheated head,
As if it mourned the something that we miss.

This pale, this over eager listening ear
The wretched mouth its soft lament to hear,
To mark the noiseless and the anguished fall
Of still one other warm misshapen tear.

Short arms, and bruised feet long set apart
To walk with us forever from the start.
Ah God, is this the reason that we love
Because such things are death blows to the heart?

To ———

Another's veins are set within my days
His misery, as much as yours, is mine
Yet tell me, is this not a virgin's gaze
Held fast in thine?

I turn always and blow the candle's flame
Into the darkness, dropping down my tears,
Striking out the ending of the game
By forty years.

And in the darkness hear the frightened moan
Of him half wounded, unidentified
Some one unutterably alone
And mystified.

Nay touch me not too tenderly or well
For I have words to every man's distress
And some forgotten ailing hand in hell
First tore this dress.

Always, yea always, always thus with me
Another's dust shall mix here, when I cease
While yours, my love, a thousand years shall be
Clotted with peace.

To the Hands of a Beloved

His hands, I love to think, have left some trace
On some white wall or dusty balustrade.
Good, eager hands, cast outward for a space
And touching things a little ere they fade
And fall and are with death anointed and dismayed.

I like to think that some day as I pass
This fall end somber mirror I shall win
The touch of his quick fingers from the glass
When, searching in his face for what had been,
He paused here utterly confounded, looking in.

On some object, unnoticed, cast aside,
Some hour he'll strike with careless palm outspread,
And there'll remain of him, though he had died.
A memory that shall lift him from the dead;
And weeping between my hands, I shall be comforted.

All-Story Cavalier Weekly, 17 May 1919, 212.

To One in Favour

When the throne stands empty, and the king goes down,
     Down into the darkness by your high white tent,
And shall sheath his gray sword, lay aside his crown;
     Then, O tall white woman, shall you be content?

Shall you be content, lying on his knee,
     Murmuring face downward, lips within his palm?
Then shall you remember, thus you once kissed me,
     Only wilder, madder, closer in my arm?

When he shall release you, turn his eyes to sleep;
     Will you lift a little, looking in his face,
And recall out parting, for a moment weep
     Down upon his doublet, tarnishing the lace?

And when up the sun rides, and the daylight comes,
     Loud with sudden sparrows, and their latest talk,
Will you take his face so, in your two long thumbs
     Kiss his mouth for kindness, then raise up and walk?

Smart Set, July 1919, 104.

To a Bird

Up from some leafy cover hot with June
      And odorous with spicy mysteries
      Of herbs unknown, a red bird dipping flies,
Whistling a little sadly, out of tune,
         Under a slow moon.

Lifts and turns, and, like blots on a wall,
      Leaves fleeting shadows in its drowsy flight;
      The earth beneath, and all above the night,
And stealing out between the last leaf's fall
         A new bird's call.

Singing its way into the South once more,
      No more returning; and the dropping leaves
      The branches strip like arms thrust out of sleeves,
And though the wind doth through the whole world roar
         A feather only stirs upon its floor.

All-Story Cavalier Weekly, 20 September 1919, 687.

To the Dead Favourite of Liu Ch'e

The sound of rustling silk is stilled.
With solemn dust the court is filled,
No footfalls echo on the floor;
A thousand leaves stop at her door,
Her little golden drink is spilled.

Her painted fan no more shall rise
Before her black barbaric eyes—
The scattered tea goes with the leaves.
And simply crossed her yellow sleeves;
And every day a sunset dies.

Her birds no longer coo and call,
The cherry blossoms fade and fall,
Nor ever does her shadow stir
But stares forever back at her,
And through her runs no sound at all.

And bending low, my falling tears
Drop fast against her little ears,
And yet no sound comes back, and I
Who used to play her tenderly
Have touched her not a thousand years.

The Dial, April 1920, 444–46. In 13.17 *Two Poems.* There is a copy in the *Approved Poems* folder in UMD. In *Intruder in the Dust* (1948), William Faulkner quoted two lines from this poem (p. 191). These are the third and fifth lines of the second stanza, which Faulkner attributes to "a small voice, a sound sensitive lady poet of the time of my youth." (The second poem here is "Pastoral," p. 81, the first poem in DB's *A Book.*)

    Commentary: DB's memoir "A Way of Life" mentions the Orientalist Arthur Waley (1889–1966), who in *A Hundred and Seventy Chinese Poems* (1919) published a translation of Liu Ch'e's poem on his dead mistress, but her source for this poem was Herbert Allen Giles, *A History of Chinese Literature* (1901, 100). Perhaps she also knew Ezra Pound's "Liu Ch'e," which was originally published in *Glebe* 1, no. 5 (February 1914) and later in *Lustra.* Pound probably saw Liu Ch'e as a very early imagist poet (Ruthven, *Guide to Ezra Pound's Personae,* 168). See introduction to this volume.

To One Feeling Differently

To-night I cannot know you and I weep
For sorrow that's upon you like soft sleep
Of which alone you are the one possessed—
And as one in long stuff of mourning dressed—
Drenched deep in garments that take shape of grief
Fold on heavy fold, as leaf on leaf.
You stand, all tremulous with stifled cries,
And with chill tears like glass upon your eyes.
Thin shadows, darker than the darkness boil
With foamy somnolence and monstrous toil
The solemn lisping of untimely things
Approaches; and on high lamenting wings
Cold time screams past us, shedding sparks of pain {fire}
Of which you are the core and the refrain.

Playboy, first quarter 1923, 36. Cf. a different version in *All-Story Weekly*, 10 July 1920, 204. There is a typed copy without changes in the *Approved Poems* folder at UMD. In "Envelope" there is a photocopy of the original, where DB wrote in 1979: "Playboy 1923 (Ahrens—not the one now on sale)." The current *Playboy* began in 1953, but there was an older magazine by that name edited by Egmont Arens that was published from January 1919 to June 1924. DB made a handwritten correction in the thirteenth line, substituting "pain" for "fire" without crossing out "fire."

She Passed This Way

Here where the trees still tremble with your flight
I sit and braid thin whips to beat you down.
How shall we ever find you who have gone
In little dresses, lisping through the town?

Great men on horses hunt you and strong boys
Employ their arrows in the shallow air.
But I shall be heard whistling where I follow
Braiding long wisps of grass and stallion's hair.

And in the night when thirty hawks are high
In pendent rhythm, and all the wayside loud;
When they are burning field and bush and hedge,
I'll steal you like a penny from the crowd.

Vanity Fair, March 1923, 14, under the general title "Two Lyrics." "The Flowering Corpse" is the ninth poem in *A Book* and is not duplicated here.

Vaudeville

Her little feet half sought the dizzy ground
And half they rose like sun motes spent in space;
A whirling rhythm in a shower of lace,
Between the music's silence and its sound.

Too frail, like cylinders of golden flake,
The curls that swing about her polished skin,
More delicate than leaf-light on a lake
The dimples that made shadows in her chin.

Ornate the Autumn with the wane of her,
The flutter of her satin-sandaled feet;
And more demure and more than quite discreet
The hem that dusts her ankles with its fur.

The light was pulsing with the quaint surprise
Of ribboned wings that aureoled her head
And like a butterfly burnt out and dead
The bister and the blue beneath her eyes.

At last she caught her spangled skirt and turned,
Taking the music's echo in its net;
And to our quick applause and quick regret
We watched the spot light empty, as it burned.

Vanity Fair, May 1923, 67. First published in *All-Story Cavalier Weekly*, 24 April 1915, 375. *Bister:* yellowish brown pigment.

Crystals

Wax-heavy, snared in age-splintered linen, the king's daughter;
The shimmer of her eyeballs blue beneath the lids like thin rain water.
Small and sour lemon blossoms banked at the breast-bone;
Her two breasts dark of death and stained a {the} dark tone.
Her lips flower-tarnished, her cheek-braids bulked in rust.
Her shoulders as hard as a wall-tree, frosted with dust.
Precise bone, clipped and grooved, and as sure as metal.
Leaf of flesh built high, like china roses, petal on petal.
Odor of apples rising from the death robes chinks and breaks.
Seeds of pepper falling down from brittle, spiced tomb-cakes.
Her swift cunning impaled on her brain's darkness. She died
Of her heart's sharp crystal spiral pricked {twisted} in her side.
Six tomb Gods in basalt make her one of these—
Who lie a million years, listening for thieves.

New Republic, 20 June 1923, 101. In box 12, folder 12. A copy of the published poem in "Envelope" has two handwritten corrections from 1979 in the fourth ("a" replaced by "the") and eleventh ("pricked" replaced by "twisted") lines.

    Commentary: When this poem was published, DB had just turned thirty-one and was living in Paris. (*A Book* was also published in 1923.) The subject matter is strangely familiar: DB takes us to the funeral of a king's daughter, presumably Chinese, lying in state surrounded by "six tomb Gods."

The Child Would Be Older

Cold tears, my brave man? Come, my little garçon,
I'll take you to my girl's breast and sing you a war song.
Where the horses gather, listen to their hoofs strike.
What is a pigeon of a scythe within the wheat like?
Oh, the single, cool thought that we string in childhood,
As clean and as brittle as a small stick of hard-wood.
Now it is a massacre, a scandal, or a penchant.
I'll cut you down a clear curl, to thicken out your swan-
song.

Shadowland, July 1923, 43.

To One in Another Mood

O dear beloved, shall I not go back
From gazing on you always with wet eyes,
And mournful kisses from these lips where lies
More honey than your aloes? Must I crack
Still darker herbs, and sighing keep the track
With feigned lamenting and with fearful cries,
Slow twining you about with blasphemies
Because I would be dancing? Nay, I lack
The needed dull intoning of despair.
Nor in me echoes your too somber mood,
Nor is it in my heart. Nor anywhere
Within my flesh the very flesh you wooed.
Then wherefore shall I loose my braided hair
Hiding my eyes, pretending that I brood?

Vanity Fair, November 1923, 118. A very similar version of this poem was published as "To One Feeling Differently" in the *All-Story Weekly*, 10 July 1920, 204. The latter title was then used for a quite different poem. Cf. p 74.

A Book and A Night Among the Horses

The eleven poems in *A Book* appear on pages 74, 103, 116, 131, 145–46, 172, 179, 194, 209, 219, and 220. In addition to the poems the volume contains three short plays, six drawings, and twelve stories. Andrew Field erroneously indicates that the "twenty short poems are distributed among the short stories of Barnes' first major book" and adds that "taken separately, they are simply poems on various themes. . . . But if eleven of them are taken out and read sequentially they constitute a story in themselves" (*Djuna*, 102). In *A Night Among the Horses*, the 1929 edition of *A Book*, the eleven poems appear without changes on pages 74, 103, 116, 131, 145–46, 172, 179, 194, 209, 258, and 259. The 1929 edition deletes the illustrations and includes three new stories, but retains the 1923 format with two poems ("First Communion" and "Finis") at the end of the book (258 and 259).

Pastoral

A frog leaps out across the lawn,
And crouches there—all heavy and alone,
And like a blossom, pale and over-blown,
Once more the moon turns dim against the dawn.

Crawling across the straggling panoply
Of little roses, only half in bloom,
It strides within that beamed and lofty room
Where an ebon stallion looms upon the hay.

The stillness moves and seems to grow immense
A shudd'ring dog starts, dragging at its chain,
Thin, dusty rats slink down within the grain,
And in the vale the first far bells commence.

Here in the dawn, with mournful doomed eyes
A cow uprises, moving out to bear
A soft-lipped calf with swarthy birth-swirled hair,
And wide wet mouth, and droll uncertainties.

The gray fowls fight for places in the sun,
The mushrooms flare, and pass like painted fans:
All the world is patient in its plans—
The seasons move forever, one on one.

Small birds lie sprawling vaguely in the heat,
And wanly pluck at shadows on their breasts,
And where the heavy grape-vine leans and rests,
White butterflies lift up their furry feet.

The wheat grows querulous with unseen cats;
A fox strides out in anger through the corn,
Bidding each acre wake and rise to mourn
Beneath its sharps and through its throaty flats.

And so it is, and will be year on year,
Time in and out of date, and still on time
A billion grapes plunge bleeding into wine
And bursting, fall like music on the ear.

The snail that marks the girth of night with slime,
The lonely adder hissing in the fern,
The lizard with its ochre eyes aburn—
Each is before, and each behind its time.

Published in *The Dial*, April 1920, 445–46, with "To the Dead Favourite of
Liu Ch'e" as "Two Poems." "Pastoral" also appeared in *Current Opinion* (August
1920, 268). There are copies of "Two Poems" in *Approved Poems*. In *Early Poems*
there is a typed poem with fragments of the first and third stanzas.

Antique

A lady in a cowl of lawn
Straight bound tabs, slow muted eyes,
Lips fair thin and deftly drawn
And oddly wise.

A cameo, a ruff of lace,
Neck cut square, with corners laid;
Long Greek nose, and by the face
A polished braid.

Low, sideways looped, of amber stain,
The pale ears caught within its snare.
A profile like a dagger lain
Between the hair.

Published in *Harper's Monthly Magazine*, August 1918, 330. In the *Early Poems* folder 8.8 *Antique* folder and in "Envelope" there are two typed clean copies with DB's "Patchin Place" address. The present editors have preferred to include the unpublished version, since it reflects DB's final choice of drafts. The main changes are in the second and seventh lines, which read "With straight-bound tabs and muted eyes" and "A thin Greek nose and near the face." She also removed the "And . . ." at the beginning of the third ("And lips . . .") and the "A . . ." at the beginning of the sixth line ("A neck . . ."). It is the only example of DB's reworking of an old poem at her Patchin Place address (DB moved there in September 1940). Here we see Djuna Barnes the portrait artist.

Hush before Love

A voice rose in the darkness saying "Love,"
And in the stall the scattered mice grew still,
Where yet the white ox slept, and on the sill
The crowing cock paused, and the grey house dove
Turned twice about upon the ledge above.

In DB's *Early Poems* folder there was a clean copy without changes except for the title, which was "Saying 'Love.'" The copy is now in the 10.17 *Saying Love!* folder.

Paradise

This night I've been one hour in Paradise;
There found a feather from the Cock that Crew—
There heard the echo of the Kiss that Slew,
And in the dark, about past agonies
            Hummed little flies.

The "cock that crew" here is, of course, a reference to the betrayal of Jesus
Christ by his disciple Peter (Matt. 26:34; 74–75), and the "kiss that slew" to
Christ's betrayal by Judas (Luke 22:47–49). These are the first of many Bib-
lical references in the poems of DB.

Six Songs of Khalidine

TO THE MEMORY OF MARY PYNE

The flame of your red hair does crawl and creep
Upon your body that denies the gloom
And feeds upon your flesh as 'twould consume
The cold precision of your austere sleep—
And all night long I beat it back, and weep.

It is not gentleness but mad despair
That sets us kissing mouths, O Khalidine,
Your mouth and mine, and one sweet mouth
        unseen
We call our soul. Yet thick within our hair
The dusty ashes that our days prepare.

The dark comes up, my little love, and dyes
Your fallen lids with stain of ebony,
And draws a thread of fear 'tween you and me
Pulling thin blindness down across our eyes—
And far within the vale a lost bird cries.

Does not the wind moan round your painted
        towers
Like rats within an empty granary?
The clapper lost, and long blown out to sea
Your windy doves. And here the black bat
        cowers
Against your clock that never strikes the hours.

And now I say, has not the mountain's base
Here trembled long ago unto the cry
"I love you, ah, I love you!" Now we die
And lay, all silent, to the earth our face.
Shall that cast out the echo of this place?

Has not one in the dark funereal
Heard foot-fall fearful, born of no man's tread,
And felt the wings of death, though no wing
        spread
And on his cheek a tear, though no tear fell—
And a voice saying without breath "Farewell!"

Khalidine means "immortal ones" in Arabic.

  Commentary: This is one of DB's best early poems, a love poem dedicated to Mary Pyne, whom DB nursed until her death of tuberculosis in 1919 (see Herring, *Djuna,* 74). The Gothic tradition is very much alive: "The flame of your red hair does crawl and creep / Upon your body that denies the gloom." The title is something of a puzzle. Beyond Mary Pyne, who are these immortals? Has the subject become immortal through memory or celebration? Is each stanza really a song? One cannot tell, but there are far more dead people than living in these early poems, and here the mood must owe something to DB's tribute to the concubine of Liu Ch'e.

Song in Autumn

The wind comes down before the creeping
        night
And you, my love, are hid within the
        green
Long grasses; and the dusk steals up between
Each leaf, as through the shadow quick with
        fright
The startled hare leaps up and out of sight.

The hedges whisper in their loaded boughs
Where warm birds slumber, pressing wing to
        wing,
All pulsing faintly, like a muted string
Above us where we weary of our vows—
And hidden underground the soft moles drowse.

Published in *Vanity Fair*, September 1923, as *Love Song in Autumn*. For *A Book*, DB changed the title and replaced some archaisms (such as "thou" for "you" and "art" for "are" in the second line). In the 8.13 *Autumn* folder there is a copy of the poem with the title changed to "Autumn" and some handwritten corrections. The "Envelope" contains a Patchin Place copy almost without changes except the title ("Nightfall").

Commentary: One steps briefly out of the mausoleum from time to time to catch a glimpse of nature and breathe some fresh air. So it is in "Song of Autumn." In autumn nature sings its song: a hare is startled, hedges whisper, birds slumber, moles drowse, and the poet's lover lies beneath the earth, hidden by long grasses.

Lullaby

When I was a young child I slept with a dog,
I lived without trouble and I thought no harm;
I ran with the boys and I played leap-frog;
Now it is a girl's head that lies on my arm.

Then I grew a little, picked plantain in the yard;
Now I dwell in Greenwich, and the people do not call;
Then I planted pepper-seed and stamped on them hard.
Now I am very quiet and I hardly plan at all.

Then I pricked my finger on a thorn, or a thistle,
Put the finger in my mouth, and ran to my mother.
Now I lie here, with my eyes on a pistol.
There will be a morrow, and another, and another.

Commentary: The ironic title here is in sharp contrast with the poem's deep despair. Memories of innocent youth contrast with contemporary suicidal anguish, the mood of a figure who would like to die, but who can't pull the trigger.

I'd Have You Think of Me

As one who, leaning on the wall, once drew
Thick blossoms down, and hearkened to the hum
Of heavy bees slow rounding the wet plum,
And heard across the fields the patient coo
Of restless birds bewildered with the dew.

As one whose thoughts were mad in painful May,
With melancholy eyes turned toward her love,
And toward the troubled earth whereunder throve
The chilly rye and coming hawthorn spray—
With one lean, pacing hound, for company.

Published in *Vanity Fair*, October 1922, 67. In *Early Poems* there are two copies with the Patchin Place address without changes except in the title ("Then Think of Her").

Commentary: Here again we have the compiling of natural images highlighting a melancholy lover with only a hound for company.

The Flowering Corpse

So still she lies in this closed place apart,
Her feet grown fragile for the ghostly tryst;
Her pulse no longer striking in her wrist,
Nor does its echo wander through her heart.

Over the body and the quiet head
Like stately ferns above an austere tomb,
Soft hairs blow; and beneath her armpits bloom
The drowsy passion flowers of the dead.

Published in *Vanity Fair*, March 1923, 14, with "She Passed This Way" as "Two Lyrics."

    Commentary: This poem brings us again the gothic modernist touch, as the poet contemplates in her imagination what may be the remains of Mary Pyne in her grave. There are sensitive, convincing images here, but also a jarring one reminiscent of Donne's "Relique," where in the lovers' grave is found "a bracelet of bright hair about the bone."

First Communion

The mortal fruit upon the bough
Hangs above the nuptial bed.
The cat-bird in the tree returns
The forfeit of his mutual vow.

The hard, untimely apple of
The branch that feeds on watered rain
Takes the place upon her lips
Of her late lamented love.

Many hands together press
Shaped within a static prayer
Recall to one the chorister
Docile in his sexless dress.

The temperate winds reclaim the iced
Remorseless vapours of the snow.
The only pattern in the mind
Is the cross behind the Christ.

Published in *The Dial*, August 1923, 166. There is a clean copy in *Approved Poems*.
    Commentary: This very obscure poem seems more like a medieval funeral for "her late lamented love" than communion in the religious sense, but despite several odd conjunctions, the images coalesce to describe a funerary mood.

Finis

For you, for me? Why then the striking hour,
The wind among the curtains, and the tread
Of some late gardener pulling at the flower
They'll lay between our hearts when we are dead.

A clean copy is in 9.9 *Finis.*

Early Unpublished Poems
(1920–25)

The first four poems ("The Poisoned Tree," "The End of Summer," "The Rose," and "Growth") are in typescript at the Houghton Library at Harvard University together with the poems published in Djuna Barnes's *A Book* (1923), some with minor changes ("First Communion" is missing), and probably date from 1920 to 1923.

The Poisoned Tree

The poisoned tree that blooms
In the orchard of my dreams
Once grew the fairest blossom.

Now a twisted nigger lives
In the shadow of its leaves.
His swollen brain's a beehive.

The earth beneath is red
Like my blood, oh, like my blood!
And seck of grass or life's seeds.

And Hate's its pendulous fruit,
Soft, ripe, and full. Here thought
Is a gathering wind . . . the root waits.

The poisoned tree that blooms
In the orchard of my dreams
Once grew the fairest blossom.

The only copy of this poem known to the editors is in the Houghton Library, Harvard University. Cf. William Blake, "A Poison Tree," from *Songs of Innocence and Experience.*

The End of Summer

Strewn seaweed ash along the beach
mark where
The land locked wind goes searching its
lost despair.

Who turns the rock of flesh today
is met
by the maggot's blind reproach, the sutler
of death.

Thin voices howling from the sea wet rock
remain unanswered in the night.
The autumn cold drifts in like fog
and coats the lawns and beach with ice,
and hides the summer coast beneath
a wavering light, a quivering fear.

The straggler turns, and turning
Wreathes smoky wraiths of smouldered yearning.

An inland bell rings out
Singing to the sea, sings out
"Are you there, and?"
"Are you there, and?"
"Are you there?"

The only copy of this poem known to the editors is in the Houghton Library,
Harvard University.

The Rose

Yes, even in this rose which I lift so lightly
There is something brooding, a darkness folded in,
Like the very best of Russian folk tales; like her
Who walked my dreams, forbidden, lost to me.

When first we met I dreamed she left a room
In which I sat, with one reluctant glance,
And with her left a man whose face was hid.
And I, alone, awoke, and saw the moon.

One evening when it snowed, we laughed, and let
It fall upon us like age. We parted laughing,
And I came home alone and dreamed of us.
But always there were people who came between,
Strangers with muffled voices and faces blurred.
When I awoke, the sun had reached high noon.

One day I saw her down the street, but not
Alone. Too far away to see his face,
I fled, and sought in sleep a dream of her.
There was no dream, but only this: a night,
Like darkness folded in a sleeping rose.

The only copy of this poem known to the editors is in the Houghton Library,
Harvard University.

Growth

Mock fallow this fearful day foregone throughout
With the toy soldiers marching, marching, marching,
And the paper zoo's menagerie howling, howling,
Let loose to spring, to snarl, to snap, to pounce.
Only the tarnished devils with glabrous tails
Who knew to work the rector-set redemption.
The child believed the carpet pattern's construction
Who cried, "I smote him thus and thus, and fairly,
And he, to see my point, admitted all.
And we had a chat—he praised me and gave
The half of his gingerbread." Her mother's love
Expended a mother's tolerant, tender smile,
Not seeing the hunk of gingerbread he held
Or the wound of paper-teeth and bayonets.
And he bled to death in sleep, and grew a man.

The only copy of this poem known to the editors is in the Houghton Library, Harvard University.

The forest tears, and lo, is seen
A brindled myth with icy mane,
Walking in a phantom dream
A vision in a vision slain.

On every branch the night moon feeds,
And still the Beast comes forth alone,
Love is burning at the heart,
Echoless and cast in stone.

Echoless by same on same
By kind to kind. The Sapphic pyre
Looms above the arctic head
Ashless and a tragic fire.

Still the Beast with wint'ry eye
Marks the shadow come and go;
Pacing down mortality
With a lost, immortal cry.

In 9.22 *Love and the Beast.* DB's Paris address, 173 boulevard Saint-Germain, appears in the upper right corner, which dates this unpublished poem as about 1923, the year in which *A Book* appeared. Apparently it was dedicated to DB's friend Natalie Clifford Barney, with whom she had a love affair before she met Thelma Wood, her lover of many years in Paris. On the page is clean type with few handwritten changes and a large handwritten question mark in the left margin, indicating to HON her possible willingness to publish the poem. In the first line "born" is crossed out and replaced by "seen." In the second line "The" is replaced by "A." In the upper left margin in DB's hand is "Be disappointed sweetly."

Commentary: "Be disappointed sweetly" is intriguing; it could refer to either lover's disappointment, but since Barney was rich, powerful, an established Parisian, and not inclined to linger long in a relationship, one may surmise that the disappointment was DB's. She was in no position to make a fuss when Barney told her that her stay was at an end and she would have to find lodging elsewhere. She had been sampled and now on to the next thing. DB never published the poem and probably did not admire it; it is merely a patron's due.

Requiem

The Sacred Heart moves to and fro.
She who was beautiful, reposes,
Lightning and thunder, the braided twain
Plunder the stars. The fallow roses
Bud against the stately rain
Death, on a milk-white ox proposes.

Unpublished from 1923. DB's Paris address on the boulevard St. Germain dates the poem. There are clean copies in 10.6 *Requiem* and 9.25 *Miscellaneous Completed* folders in UMD and in "Envelope." In the *Miscellaneous Completed* copy, "ox" in the last line is not crossed out but has "ass" and "donkey" handwritten underneath.

Commentary: Somehow one is not surprised to find a poem called "Requiem" in DB's lengthening chapbook of morbidity, but one remembers too that these poems are also a measure of the depth of her feeling of loss. Her mother was right when she wrote to DB: "You have condensed your agony until its pure platinum . . ." (Elizabeth Barnes to DB, 1 December 1936 [UMD]). Published separately as they were, the graveside poems make a rather more poignant impression than they do collected together as "Early Poems." At the end of her life, DB would return to her early taste for the graveyard muse, but there her poems are quite different, being hard, intellectual, and metaphysical.

Portrait of a Lady Walking

In the North birds feather a long wind.
She is beautiful.
The Fall lays ice on the lemon's rind.
Her slow ways are attendant on the dark mind.
The frost sets a brittle stillness on the pool.
Onto the cool short pile of the wet grass
Birds drop like a shower of glass.

Unpublished from 1924–25 in the 9.25 *Miscellaneous Completed* and 10.3 *Portrait of a Lady Walking* folders. Clean typed copy signed "Djuna Barnes, 'Le Colombier' Cagnes sur mer, (A. M.) France," with a handwritten note: "Turned down by Marianne Moore when Editor of the 'Dial.'" DB was in Cagnes-sur-Mer with Thelma Wood from 14 October 1924 until 16 February 1925. Marianne Moore was editor of *The Dial* from July 1926 to July 1928.

Commentary: Here the poet is observing a live woman and in so doing creates one of the best of the early poems.

Galerie Religieuse

Stampede in the Resurrection.
Do you think, would you say, there'd be a stampede in the Resurrection?

The brief boys in their holy laces,
Sing the toneless scale in pleasant voices,
With edgeless well-water faces.
In ponderous herds, the Great Bishops volley
Hosanna home, with head as heavy as a church, lowing oblivion.
Shadows boil the vaults, and burst
Spilling darkness down upon the altar,
Time rots upon the stem of night and day.

Unpublished from 1924–25, this poem has the Cagnes-sur-Mer address. It can be found in 9.12 *Galerie Religieuse* and "Envelope." This is a single copy with a few handwritten corrections. Compare this poem to the 1962 poem of the same title, which appears in the Late Published section of this volume.

Commentary: This earlier version envisions the Resurrection as a stampede of choirboys and bishops "lowing hosannas" as graves of the faithful empty out. There is wit here, and altogether a better mood than in most of the earlier poems. It is in sharp contrast with the agony implicit in Nora's vision of the Resurrection in *Nightwood,* by which reference she pays a supreme compliment to her parting lover: "In the resurrection, when we come up looking backward at each other, I shall know you only of all that company" (58–59).

Archaic

Sleep the slain white bull.
The stars unbud upon the seven pillars.
Behind the thunder cries the heavy bird.
(The crying bird cries behind the cloud.)
The Lost Enigma lies upon his bier.
His fluted robes a funnel of fate.
The lilies in the field give back no light.
The cold bell in the tower rains on the shields.

Ca. 1924–25, unpublished. The various drafts are now in an individual folder at UMD: box 9, folder 10. An earlier version contained this address: "Djuna Barnes, 'Le Colombier' Traverse du General Beranger, Cagnes—A.M. France." The editors have chosen to present here a later, relatively clean version that includes her mother's address: "Djuna Barnes, % Mrs. E. C. Barnes, 501 Park Avenue, East Orange, New Jersey."

Death and the Wood

The stricken bird, upon her tomb of eggs
Grips that sepulchre with rocking legs,
Where once the hot core of her vision sealed
Now glacial pivot of an outer cold
The iris splintered with a sudden frost
Of time's javelins and the host
That bar the panting of her kill
Pouring forth her panting and the kill
Death, threads and shuttles her silent song
Death heaves up her wing, death makes her sing
Death turns her everywhere about around
Death sits on her wing
Death is her song, My Lord
Death gates her the cockpit of the windless tail
The worm heaves her everywhere abroad.

Cf. "Death Betrayal in the Wood" (box 8, folder 17) in new UMD catalog. Undated. In "Envelope" in DB's hand appears "Only for use of possible lines," a notation of ca. 1978. The seventh and eighth lines look like variants, but both are cleanly typed. "The maggot fastens on her breastbone meat" is typed at the top of the page. Two related versions begin with "the stricken thrush" and have twenty-two lines.

Zadel Barnes Gustafson (1841–1917), grandmother of Djuna Barnes. Photo dated 1891. (Barnes Family Papers, Special Collections, University of Maryland Libraries)

Elizabeth Chappell Barnes (1862–1945), mother of Djuna Barnes. (Papers of Djuna Barnes, Special Collections, University of Maryland Libraries)

Wald Barnes (1865–1934), father of Djuna Barnes. Photo dated October 1889. (Papers of Djuna Barnes, Special Collections, University of Maryland Libraries)

Djuna Barnes and brother Thurn (1890–1978). (Papers of Saxon Barnes, Special Collections, University of Maryland Libraries)

Djuna Barnes as a young girl. (Papers of Djuna Barnes, Special Collections, University of Maryland Libraries)

Djuna Barnes, May 1904, age 11. (Papers of Djuna Barnes, Special Collections, University of Maryland Libraries)

Djuna Barnes, May 1906, age 13. (Papers of Djuna Barnes, Special Collections, University of Maryland Libraries)

Djuna Barnes, July 1909, age 17. Otto Sarony Studio. (Papers of Djuna Barnes, Special Collections, University of Maryland Libraries)

Djuna Barnes, Christmas 1914, age 22. (Papers of Djuna Barnes, Special Collections, University of Maryland Libraries)

Djuna Barnes in the 1920s. Photo by Berenice Abbott. (Papers of Djuna Barnes, Special Collections, University of Maryland Libraries; used by permission of Commerce Graphics)

Mary Pyne of the Provincetown Players, ca. 1915. (Papers of Djuna Barnes, Special Collections, University of Maryland Libraries)

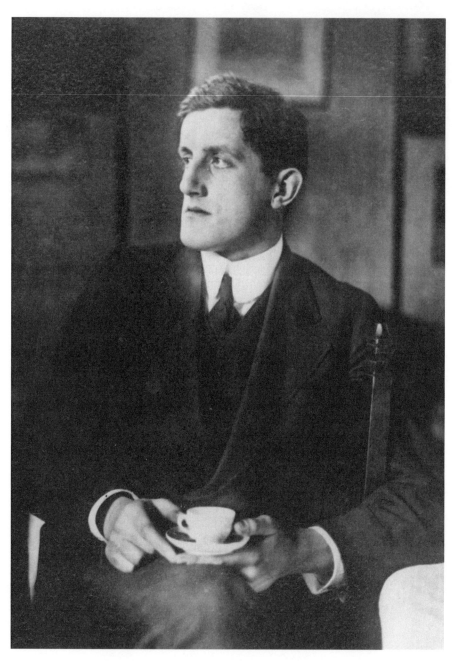

Ernst "Putzi" Hanfstaengl (1887–1975). Photo dated 1911. (Papers of Saxon Barnes, Special Collections, University of Maryland Libraries)

Djuna Barnes, 1921–22, age 29 or 30. Photo by Emil Hoppe. (Papers of Djuna Barnes, Special Collections, University of Maryland Libraries)

Thelma Wood (1901–70). (Papers of Djuna Barnes, Special Collections, University of Maryland Libraries)

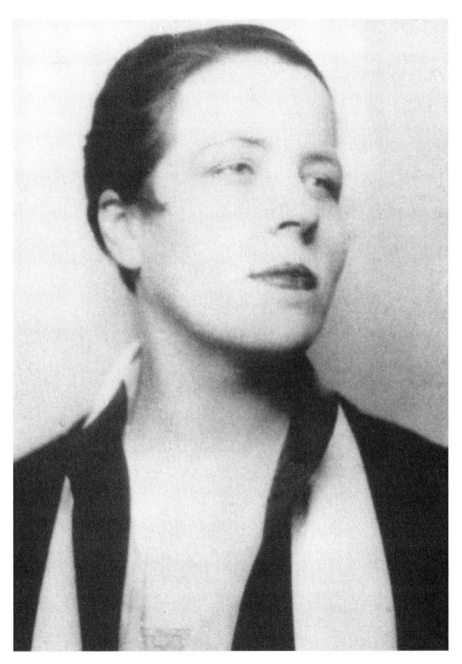

Djuna Barnes as young woman. (Papers of Djuna Barnes, Special Collections, University of Maryland Libraries)

Djuna Barnes in early middle age. (Papers of Djuna Barnes, Special Collections, University of Maryland Libraries)

Djuna Barnes, early 1970s, about age 80. (Papers of Djuna Barnes, Special Collections, University of Maryland Libraries)

Djuna Barnes, from *The Book of Repulsive Women.* (Papers of Djuna Barnes, Special Collections, University of Maryland Libraries)

Djuna Barnes, "One Gentleman Immediately Started a Cry of 'There's a Specimen,' and Kept It Up for the Rest of the Afternoon," *New York Tribune,* 16 February 1919. In Douglas Messerli, ed., *Poe's Mother.* (Papers of Djuna Barnes, Special Collections, University of Maryland Libraries)

"The portion of dramatic art that locates in the small of the back."

Djuna Barnes, "The portion of dramatic art that locates in the small of the back." Illustration for "David Warfield—Optimist," *New York Morning Telegraph Sunday Magazine*, 14 January 1917. (Papers of Djuna Barnes, Special Collections, University of Maryland Libraries)

Djuna Barnes,
5,Patchin Place,
New York,N.Y. IOOII.

September I,I974.

Viaticum.

Should any ask whose bail her tender got,
To the profit of what parasite be fed

To what parasite,what predator be feed
This ancient wrack,this cattle faced pucelle
To whom bequeathe? She being her own last vehicle
A sparrow still flying in her teeth?
Dante said,when the body fell,the bones alome were staid;
But what of the three hundred bones of the maid?
The three hundred and the third

Jaw-bone of The Word?
Primum mobile, meeting the immovable
And nothing said?
No word? impossible! equivocal
Tertium quid, diabolical— invisible
Then to whom bequeathe? on
She being her own last vehicle?
From what quietus take?
This worm that flies to justice, naked and alone..   Viaticum?
Be brief
Say Phaethon, who stood in fail
Upon the leaf,
Say Dameon who who stayed.
The worm that flies to justice, naked and alone—
Viaticum?
Re-brief—

A draft of Djuna Barnes's poem "Viaticum," dated 1 September 1974. (Papers of Djuna Barnes, Special Collections, University of Maryland Libraries)

Late Published Poems
(1938–82)

The hiatus between the last of the early poems and the first of the late ones (1929 to 1938) is explained in large part by Barnes's concentration on her novel *Nightwood*.

Transfiguration

The prophet digs with iron hands
Into the shifting desert sands.

The insect back to larva goes;
Struck to seed the climbing rose.

To Moses' empty gorge, like smoke
Rush inward all the words he spoke.

The knife of Cain lifts from the thrust;
Abel rises from the dust.

Pilate cannot find his tongue;
Bare the tree where Judas hung.

Lucifer roars up from earth;
Down falls Christ into his death.

To Adam back the rib is plied,
A creature weeps within his side.

Eden's reach is thick and green;
The forest blows, no beast is seen.

The unchained sun, in raging thirst,
Feeds the last day to the first.

London Bulletin no. 3 (June 1938): 2. The *Bulletin* was a publication of the British surrealists (it published its last issue, nos. 18–20, in June 1940). 13.16 *Transfiguration*. There are other versions of this poem in the 11.5 *Transfiguration* folder and clean typed copies in the 9.4 *Faber & Faber* folder at UMD. It is no. 28 in "List" (see O'Neal, "*Life is painful*," 92–95). A revised copy of the poem was published in 1978 in Germain, *Surrealist Poetry in English*, 156. In the *Faber & Faber* folder there is clean typed copy of this revised copy. The editors have chosen to include only the 1978 version as DB's final choice of drafts. The differences between the 1938 and the 1978 version include: first line, "claws" is replaced by "hands"; second line, "the desert's sinking floors" is replaced by "the drifting desert sands"; tenth line, "Judas climbs the tree he hung" is replaced by "Bare the tree where Judas hung." And in the fourteenth line "woman" is replaced by "creature." See also the next poem, "Fall-out over Heaven."

Commentary: Gone are the weepy graveside poems of the early years, and present are the hard, intellectual, often quite brilliant poems worthy of the author of *Nightwood,* a book where, as here, one often finds language so stressed that it overreaches denotative meaning. It is no accident that the first of these late poems appeared in publications of British surrealists, for there is definitely surrealism in the mix of many of DB's late poems. She puts the maximum stress on language to capture a deeper personal, sometimes witty vision of life, death, and the human enterprise. "Transfiguration" is an exciting poem that envisions a cataclysmic event, perhaps earth's final moments; several lines were recycled into "Fall-out over Heaven," where the event is obviously nuclear destruction. In 1938, when "Transfiguration" was published, the atom bomb had, of course, not yet been invented, but twenty years later everybody was worried about it. Both versions provide a religious context for the apocalyptic event; the second version was a tribute to T. S. Eliot on his seventieth birthday.

Fall-out over Heaven

I'll show you fear in a handful of dust.
　　　　—*The Waste Land*, line 30

And dust shall be the serpent's meat.
　　　　—Isaiah: lxv.25

The atom, broken in the shell,
Licks up Eden's reach, and Hell.

To Adam back his rib is thrown,
A mole of woman quakes, undone.

From the ground the knife of Cain
Slays the brother it has slain.

To Moses' empty gorge, like smoke
Rush backward all the words he spoke.

Lucifer roars up from earth.
Down falls Christ into his death . . .

She, supposing him to be the gardener . . .
　　　　—John: xx.15

Appeared in Braybrooke, *T. S. Eliot*, 27. The text is identical to the clean copy signed "Djuna Barnes for TSE [70th birthday]" in 8.9 *Approved Poems* and "Envelope." Other versions appear in 9.5 *Fall-Out.* Related to "Transfiguration" (1938). The first epigraph is the thirtieth line from Eliot's poem ("I will show you . . ."). Cf. Ecclesiastes 12:7: "Then shall the dust return to the earth as it was: and the spirit shall return unto God who gave it." In one version the fourth line reads "His mole of woman in his side" (11.5 *Transfiguration* folder). DB's biblical quotations are from the King James Version (1611).

Galerie Religieuse

The blood of the Lamb and the oriflamme
Wax and wane in the raked heart's core.
Hell flowers lightly; an angel slain
And cropped of earth, twines with the twain.
Above the arc of the icy laces,
In long sheaved wings, the heavenly choir,
With lambent, fourfold, impending faces
Shout upward through the motes of prayer,
Shaking the ranks of stately lilies,
In *Saint Denis*, where His Love is spent,
Dwindling on the mouth of Time,
Spiked on the votive thorn of Lent.

Ramparts 1, no. 3 (November 1962): 17. An earlier version was published in a book also edited by Neville Braybrooke, *The Wind and the Rain: An Easter Book for 1962*, 290. It is poem no. 27 in "List." Two clean copies are to be found in 9.12 *Galerie Religieuse*, similar to the 1962 book text; one has two handwritten notes: "Sent to Braybrooke for *The Wind & The Rain* (London) June 4–60" and "Corrected in N.Y. publication *Ramparts*." The present editors used the *Ramparts* version, which is clearly later, rather than the book version. The *Ramparts* text is similar to the one that accompanies the Italian translation by C. C. (Cristina Campo) in *Conoscenza Religiosa*, a magazine edited by Elémire Zolla, with whom DB had abundant correspondence. The main changes in the *Ramparts* version are in the sixth line, from "The long shaved wings of the heavenly choir" to "In long shaved wings. The heavenly choir." There are five clean copies in 8.9 *Approved Poems*, all with the *Ramparts* sixth line. In one copy there is a change in the tenth line, "In Saint Denis, where His love is spent"; "His" is crossed out (this copy also has a handwritten note by DB: "Printed in 'Ramparts'—196–?"). The reference is to the Basilica of Saint Denis in Paris, mentioned in DB's narrative "A Way of Life." The oriflamme is the red or orange/red flag of the abbey at Saint-Denis. One copy is marked "UK group" (on this designation, see p. xviii) and another copy has a handwritten note: "I think in 'Ramparts' a long time ago." DB remembered correctly, and the *Ramparts* version is the definitive one. The 9.12 *Galerie Religieuse* folder also contains a version of "Galerie Religieuse" written in 1924–25, which is included in the Early Unpublished Poems section.

Commentary: In the 1962 version one finds what seems to be a powerful, obscure reading of a religious painting that may have caught the poet's imagination at the Abbey at Saint-Denis. From first to last, one sees considerable development in DB's poetic skill.

Quarry

While I unwind duration from the tongue-tied tree,
Send carbon fourteen down for time's address.
The old revengeful without memory
Stand by:
I come, I come that path and there look in
And see the capsized eye of sleep and wrath
And hear the beaters' "Gone to earth!"
Then do I sowl the soul and strike its face
That it fetch breath.

New Yorker, 27 December 1969, 53. Reprinted in 1972 in *A Festschrift for Djuna Barnes on Her 80th Birthday* (ed. A. Gildzen), where the poem opens the book. This version, selected by the present editors, has two changes from the *New Yorker* text: DB replaces a dash with a colon in the fourth line and "slap" with "strike" in the eighth line (DB's copy of the *Festschrift* at UMD has a handwritten note: "amended"). The *New Yorker* copy is in box 13, folder 16. The 10.4 *Quarry* folder at UMD contains a clean copy of the poem with a caption "Published in the New Yorker as of December 27, 1969" and a footnote: "Corrected in the fourth line, colon, not a dash. And in the last line but one, 'strike' in place of 'slap.' I think you will have to ask The New Yorker for permission to reproduce this poem. I'm not sure this might not mess up any other ports I might dock in?" Signed by hand "D.B." This copy has another handwritten note by DB: "Copy sent to Mrs [unreadable four-letter name] of New Dir." The poem is no. 45 in "List." The 10.4 *Quarry* folder at UMD has some previous versions and clean copies marked "O.K" and "German group." Some copies have the general title of "Poems in Progress." An undated copy has the "OK" mark and the title "Quarry" is crossed out and replaced by "Epitaph." There are other versions of the poem in other folders (such as 8.10 and 11 *As Cried* and 10.13 to 16 *Satires*), sometimes as stanzas in longer poems. In the *Quarry* folder there are three other copies identical to the 1969 published text, but with "slap" replaced by "strike" in the eighth line, which is the text published in the 1972 *Festschrift*. Concerning "sowl the soul" in the eighth line, DB told HON that "If you don't know the meaning of 'sowl' it is impossible to figure out the ending of the poem" (*"Life is painful,"* 43). It is clear that DB uses "sowl" in its archaic meaning as shaking the head of an animal or human with your hands (*OED*), as used in *Coriolanus* 4.5.198: "He'll go, he says, and sowl the porter of Rome's gates by the ears." Scientists use carbon-14 dating radioactivity to determine the age of objects or human remains.

Commentary: This is a beautifully complex poem about winding down our personal spool of fate until we reach death's door. The speaker "unwinds duration" by reference to the rings of a tree and the carbon-14 dating process but envisions vengeful elements awaiting the dying pilgrim, and also the task of striking life into the soul just as babies are spanked in the delivery room. The poem has a Yeatsian quality of gyres and human fate.

The Walking-Mort

Call her walking-mort; say where she goes
She squalls her bush with blood. I slam a gate.
Report her axis bone it gigs the rose.
What say of mine? It turns a grinning grate.
Impugn her that she baits time with an awl.
What do my sessions then? They task a grave.
So, shall we stand, or shall we tread and wait
The mantled lumber of the buzzard's fall
(That maiden resurrection and the freight),
Or shall we freeze and wrangle by the wall?

Published in the *New Yorker*, 15 May 1971, 34. It is no. 7 in "List" with the com-
ment "first part of 'Dereliction,' then 'Discant,' O.K." There are copies marked
"OK" in 8.9 *Approved Poems* and in the 9.4 *Faber & Faber* folders. Different ver-
sions of this poem appear in several folders (*As Cried* and *Satires*). The 11.12
Walking Mort folder has sixteen versions of the poem dated between 1966 and
1970. These versions have changes, especially in the second line, where "squalls"
is replaced by "qualls," "scalds," or "squills." Two copies have changes in the
title. In one the title is crossed out and replaced by "Dulcinia" in red ink. In
another there are three possible typed titles: "Image de Espagnol [*sic*]," "Motif
Espagnole," and "Spanish Landscape." In 8.12 *As Cried*, there is a page dated
28 August 1966, where the poem has an additional last line that is crossed out:
"Say there's something Spanish in it all." It appears as spoken by Dan (the
narrator). Many versions suggest that the poem published in 1971 is part of
the *As Cried* cycle, and in some there is actually a dialog between Dan and
Nelly Hauk/Hook, who is "the mort" (*OED* gives "a walking mort" as a
1592 example for "mort" meaning loose woman). The Dan character (Dan
Corbeau or Dan Corve or Corvo or Casper Corvo or Don Coeue or Dom
Corbé or Dan Brisk or Dan Smart or Dan Apparent or Dan Pasquin, and so
on, names that appear in almost all folders, especially *As Cried, Jackdaw, Laugh-
ing Lamentations, The Ponder Rose, Rakehell, Tom Fool,* and *Satires*) has two interlocu-
tors: (1) Josquin Coustance-Custom-Custeau (in the prose memoirs included
in this volume, "the Josquin" is the devil) and (2) Nelly Hauk or Houk or
Hook (Della Houk, Della Van Hook, Hortense Corve, Bella Houk the Rich
Rag-Picker of Milan). In 9.21 *Laughing Lamentations*, there is a series of poems

called *The Cantos of Dan,* dated 25 September 1964. In all these poems Dan seems to work as a spokesman for DB. Cf. Dr. Matthew O'Connor in *Nightwood,* a character inspired by Dan Mahoney (1880?–1956).

Commentary: The title reminds us of DB's love of all-but-forgotten terms, in this case one for the prostitute. Yet it is also ambiguous, because we all, if ambulatory, are walking to our graves as time's spool winds down. At one end a fence encloses Patchin Place, where DB lived for the last forty years of her life, and it is perhaps a gate in this fence that the poet slams against the prostitute, while still realizing their shared mortality. The axis bone is the second cervical vertebra, on which the head turns; perhaps metaphorically it gigs the rose in death or is envisioned to do so. The walking-mort walks her way as do we all, awaiting "the buzzard's fall," so perhaps it is not for us to judge her. Line 7: "tread" here may mean "copulation"; cf. Shakespeare's play *Love's Labour Lost,* 5.2.187: "To tread a measure with you in the grass."

Creatures in an Alphabet

Alas!

⁓

When hovering, the Hummingbird
Is always going home (it's said).
By flying in a single spot
It's striving fast to think it's not.

⁓

With cloven lip, with baleful eye,
The Camel wears the caliph high.
But though he do the master's will,
He himself's his habit still.

⁓

Why is it the Donkey haws,
And backs away (the mule) because
Although it hasn't said it's who,
It's practicing *solfeggio.*

⁓

The reason that the Elephant
Is both detained and yet at ease,
Is because it is four trees
That the Lord forgot to plant.

⁓

The Fish, the Fish, how is he caught?
With grave intent, or so we thought;
Yet with what a flattened look
It goes fishing, without hook.

⁓

The trim Giraffe, on ankles slight,
Dips its crown in pale moonlight;
But what it poles for, none can say—
It's much too up and high away.

∽

The Hippo is a wading junk,
A sort of Saratoga trunk
With all its trappings on its back,
Through which the birds of passage peck.

∽

When from mischief interdict,
The Imago perfected rise,
And lays its dool at Heaven's Gate,
Then in this alphabet it is.

∽

Though it be loud with auguries
Of summer sun, and happy days;
Nonetheless the Blue Jay is
Lined with insect agonies.

∽

The Kinkajou, the hanging sloth,
Or any else that looks uncouth,
Aren't they somewhat upside down?
Or are they merely three of both?

∽

Horrid hunger is the cause,
That opens up the Lion's jaws;
Yet what it tears apart for meat
Is merely what its victims ate.

∽

In the zoo the Monkeys screech
At any dainty out of reach;
Yet let a corpulence be found,
They whack it madly to the ground.

∾

If ascension is your hope,
Ride not the Nigor (antelope)
But mount the springbok for the run;
It jumps straight up, like hot popcorn

∾

When musing on the Ocelot,
Or on the panther's hurling tail,
One wonders how such stealth is caught,
And how it be the cats prevail.

∾

If among itself it go,
(As the Peacock's said to do),
With all its thousand eyes ajar,
Is it itself it's looking for?

∾

Now for quidnunc, now for Quail,
(One runs off, the others rail);
But what about? It ends the same—
An old man's titter, a young man's game.

∾

What of Raccoon, animal?
With visor down (or domino),
When at *ombre* or *quadrille*,
Will it vail and let you know?

∾

The Seal, she lounges like a bride,
Much too docile, there's no doubt;
Madame Récamier, on side,
(If such she has), and bottom out.

∾

"Tyger! Tyger!"—Who wrote that?
You won't take it with your hat,
Nor lure it with a golden cage;
It won't leap its master's page.

~

Unicorn, the one-horned beast
Mistranslated from the start,
(See Deuteronomy, at least),
An upright, but a much vex'd art.

~

Now of the Vesper Wasp beware,
Its butt and bust hang by an hair,
Its sting's a death; otherwise
It's riggish in its enterprise.

~

—Somewhat sullen, many days,
The Walrus is a cow that neighs.
Tusked, ungainly, and windblown,
It sits on ice, and alone.

~

As there was nothing more to say,
The X has crossed himself away.
And as there's nothing new to prove,
He marked his exit with his love.

~

A bale of hair, the Yak he be,
His bitter butter minged in tea;
With all his craggy services,
His lowly life Himalayan is.

The present editors consulted the first edition (*Creatures in an Alphabet* [New York: Dial Press, 1982). The book, dedicated to Emily Coleman, appeared in October 1982, four months after DB's death. It was written around 1971–78 at the urging of the editor Fran McCullough, who was involved in the 1972 edition of *Ladies Almanack* by Harper & Row, and HON, who corrected the galley proofs (O'Neal, *"Life is painful,"* 41, 161). The draft that DB worked on with O'Neal in November 1978 was dated from 1971 (*"Life is painful,"* 41). In February 1979 she "settle[d] on two titles: *The Rite of Spring* for the major poem and *Figures in an Alphabet* for the animal verses" (*"Life is painful,"* 63). The book is a bestiary in the medieval tradition with twenty-six rimed quatrains (in reality twenty-five because for the *A* the text reads only "Alas!"): An introductory poem, *B* is "hummingbird," *C* "camel," *D* "donkey," *E* "elephant," *F* "fish," *G* "giraffe," *H* "hippo," *I* "the imago," *J* "blue jay," *K* "kinkajou," *L* "lion," *M* "monkey," *N* "nigor," *O* "ocelot," *P* "peacock," *Q* "quail," *R* "raccoon," *S* "seal," *T* "tyger," *U* "unicorn," *V* "vespers Wasp," *W* "walrus," *X* an apology to no animal, and *Y* "yak." There is no poem for *Z*; perhaps she could think of no poem about a zebra or zebu. The poems have no titles. After the dedication is a quatrain:

The adder in the grass can hiss
The lynxes in the dark can kiss
Each otter holds his otter's hand
For this is how the Lord has planned.

And a line at the end of the book: "Round the mulberry we go."

Commentary: The poems in this slight volume were not tossed off in an afternoon; DB labored hard over them in her late eighties because they brought in a little money. Hank O'Neal remembers her working on them. He says in a diary entry for 17 November 1978, "We worked on the animal poems. She is now satisfied with the first six verses but does not want any to be printed unless they are all up to the standards of the seal and the giraffe. She is having trouble with the letter 'I.' We went through various dictionaries looking for animals and unusual words with little success" (*"Life is painful,"* 47). One can surely imagine DB surrounded by medieval or Renaissance dictionaries and the *OED*, using her natural wit to find something clever to say about one animal per letter.

Rite of Spring

Man cannot purge his body of its theme
As can the silkworm on a running thread
Spin a shroud to re-consider in.

Grand Street 1, no. 3 (Spring 1982): 66. The first poem of the 10.7 *Rite of Spring* folder at UMD is a clean typescript of the three-line poem, dated 25 May 1980, similar to the published poem, with a typed one-line commentary: "Twenty years trying to finish this poem." Another clean copy of the three-line poem, undated, has a long note that describes DB's poetics at that time: "Submitted to 'The New Yorker.' A totally new idea, as a poem 'in progress,' as Joyce's 'Work in Progress' was to become 'Finnegans Wake.' Tho Howard Moss, (poetry editor of that magazine) was too stupid to see. He wanted it, but only if I would change one word. I would not. Thus the booby Moss was too stupid to see, and lost the first new move, in poetry, a poem waiting, to be continued." The notion of "a totally new idea" is repeated in a letter to Fran McCullough, dated 10 March 1982 (DB died 19 June 1982). A possible clue to the silkworm image is given in a marginal note in an unrelated poem ("Laughing Lamentations of Corbeau," page dated 6 January 1966, in 9.19 *Laughing Lamentations*). DB quotes from Joseph Addison (1672–1719): "The silkworm after having spun her task, lays her eggs and dies." In 10.7 *Rite of Spring* there is a version similar to the published text (except for commas in the second and third lines) with a handwritten note: "For Saxon's attention: April 10, 1981—so far unfinished. D.B." Saxon Barnes was the youngest of her brothers and the one with whom she was most in contact. There is also a commentary by Saxon written in pencil: "Profound farewell to man." The editors have included a reworked draft of this poem in "Dereliction (Man cannot purge . . .)." The title may derive from Igor Stravinsky's ballet *Le Sacre du printemps* (1913).

Commentary: This poem was recycled into poems with other titles, such as "Dereliction (Man cannot purge . . .)." She loved these lines: "Man cannot purge his body of its theme / As can the silkworm on a running thread / Spin a shroud to reconsider in." What was she imagining man's theme to be? The silkworm lives to make its silk, reproduce, and die. The theme of humanity is perhaps to wonder why. As a group, the late published poems comprise the best that DB ever published—they are certainly the most polished—but as we shall see, there were treasures in the drafts hardly less intriguing that for clarity make these published poems seem easy work to comprehend.

Late Unpublished Poems
(CA. 1950–82)

Dereliction (Man cannot purge . . .)

Man cannot purge his body of its theme,
As goes the silkworm ferrying her thread,
To baste a shroud to metamorphose in
From a silk-proud mouth
But no sanctuary in the fossil's eye,
Pander, pass by.

In 8.19 *Dereliction.* Related to no. 19 in "List" and to "Rite of Spring," the last poem in the Late Published Poems section. There are three versions of the poem dated 30 May, 31 May, and 1 June 1971; the version used here is from 1 June. The first line is similar to the first line of "Rite of Spring," and the fifth line becomes the first line of a series of poems, some included in the *There is no gender in the fossil's eye* folder. In the 30 May version, the fifth line has "gender," in the 31 May version "quarter," replaced by handwritten "sanctuary" in the 1 June version.

    Commentary: This poem is a reworking of "Rite of Spring" and seems to be still in the draft state; the last two lines seem unconnected to the previous four.

Satires (Man cannot purge . . .)

Man cannot purge his body of its theme,
As does the silk-worm ferry forth her thread,
High Commander, tell me what is man
And what surmise?
Is breast milk in the lamentation yet?
O predacious victim of the wheel,
St. Catherine of roses, turn your gaze
Where woe is;
Purge the body of its dread,
As does the bombace from her furnace heave
To weave a shroud to metamorphose in?
To re-consider in
What bolt of havoc holds your dread?
On what cast of terror are you fed?

In 10.13 *Satires.* Related to no. 19 in "List," but with the exception of the first
two lines, it is a very different poem. Included on page 12 of a thirteen-page-
long poem or "canto" dated May 1968, of which there are three copies.
Copy 1 is thirteen pages long and is a clean copy with few corrections. Copy
2 is twelve pages long with the title "Satires of Dan Pasquin" typed with
"Dan Pasquin" crossed out and replaced by "Dom Foxtus"; then both titles
are crossed out. This copy also has a note on the title page: "copies of one
sent to [Peter] Sautoy 6 May 1968." The poem has only seven handwritten
corrections and is the text included here. Copy 3 has eleven pages with the
"Satires of Dan Pasquin" title crossed out; the twelfth page of the poem is
misplaced in the 8.18–19 *Dereliction* folder. In "Envelope," the "List" item
no. 19 consists of two copies of a two-stanza poem dated 13 July 1978. The
first stanza is identical to the "Rite of Spring" published poem, and the
second stanza is twenty-one lines long. In 10.7 *Rite of Spring* there are later ver-
sions, one dated 16 February 1980 (with a sixteen-line second stanza), and the
other dated 23 February 1980 marked "OK?" with a sixteen-line second stanza.
As the poems are now arranged, the "what is man" theme begins in "Satires
(Man cannot . . .)," continues into other poems such as "The Rounds,"
"Laughing Lamentations (Lord, what is man . . .)," and "As Cried (Lord, what
is man . . .)." Since the word "Lord" generally precedes the phrase, the source

is biblical (Psalms 8:4–6 and Hebrews 2:6); but in the simpler form the "What is man?" reference could be made to many sources, including Job 7:17, Ecclesiastes 6:11, Shakespeare's *All's Well that Ends Well,* and Byron's "Don Juan."

Commentary: In this poem we see a more concerted effort by DB to bring focus to the "man cannot purge" theme. The poem has now grown to fourteen lines, many quite intriguing.

The Bo Tree

All children, at some time, and hand in hand
Go to the woods to be un-parented
And ministered in the leaves. The frozen bole
The spirit kicks in spring, will that amend
The winter in the hearse? Pick from his hole
The daub was Caesar? Will the damned
Who rake the sparrows bones the fires burn black,
Find the pilgrims down, a tree stuck in their back?

In 8.9 *Approved Poems.* Two identical clean copies (one marked "O.K." by DB
and "German Group" by HON). The original title is "The Tree" and "Bo"
is handwritten in both copies. No. 1 in "List." The poem belongs to the *Dere-
liction* group, although it also appears in other groups (8.10–11 *As Cried*, 10.13–16
Satires, and 11.9–11 *Virgin Spring*). In some copies in 11.9 *Virgin Spring* the poem
is a stanza in longer poems and appears as "The Bodhi Tree" or "The Tree
of Heaven." The bo tree, or pipal, is the fig tree (*Ficus religiosa*) of India held
sacred by the Buddhists, who believe that Gautama received enlightenment
under a bo tree at Bodh Gaya. *Bombace:* cotton wadding.

    Commentary: This poem begins as if one were following the path of Hänsel
and Gretel into the forest, but then one encounters a list of questions having
to do with mortality, the loss of parents, perhaps even the betrayal of children
by parents, which is the theme of DB's *The Antiphon.* In the poem's last line
the speaker asks if "the damned" will find the pilgrims, such as Buddha was,
with a tree stuck in their (collective?) back, perhaps as punishment for their
wish to discover enlightenment.

Lament for Wretches, Every One

As whales by dolphins slashed, bring on a school
Of lesser fins to passenger the blood,
So comes my general man, both my priest, and hood
To ask, "who drank baptism down in nothing flat?
Who cut the comb in half to see it quick
With buzzing backsides, quartered out of cells?
And sick
And staggered regents staling pedestals?"
I replied:
"What heard of Darkness oysters in your tide?"

9.25 in *Miscellaneous Completed Poems.* No. 3 in "List." Clean copy with only two changes by hand. There are different versions in the 8.10–11 *As Cried,* 11.4 *Tom Fool,* and 10.13–16 *Satires* folders. In the tenth line "heart" is corrected by hand as "heard," which is an archaism for herdsman, heard groom, shepherd. The line perhaps alludes to Joseph Conrad's *Heart of Darkness. Staling:* in one version of the poem dated 31 July 1966, Tom Fool mentions "pissing pedestals."

Commentary: At the beginning of the poem there is a comparison between whales, slashed and bleeding, and "my general man." The man asks another series of questions that seem to have no answers but are beautifully absurd: "Who drank baptism down in nothing flat?" (Who ever drank baptismal waters?) Who cut into a honeycomb to see the "buzzing backsides" of bees. (Is there some connection with baptism?) Has one heard of "sick and staggered regents staling pedestals"? To these questions there is a reply at the poem's end, really another question: "What heard of Darkness oysters in your tide?" These lines have a certain power, and DB must have loved the words, so perhaps we are to admire the surreal beauty and power of this vision. The poem is both complete and polished as it stands, in contrast to others that seem inconclusive.

Dereliction (There are no sessions . . .)

There are no sessions in a fossils eye,
Pander, pass by.

The great meadow sarcophagus, the tomb
Great monuments to lay the forehead on
Monuments for sheep to lay the forehead on
Lays the face away, but not for buriel?
There are no seasons in a fossils eye—
Up from her coign of banishment,
Up from her steep delay
Comes Io on her arms a field away.

In 8.20 *Dereliction* related to no. 29 in "List."

Descant (There is no gender . . .)

  Pro vita sua

Of Dereliction, Parthenogenesis and Phantom {Victim} Spring

There is no gender in a fossil's eye,
Pander, pass by.

Should any ask whose bale her tender mark
Be brief,
Say Phaeton who stood in fail
Upon a leaf;
Say Endymion who snored,
Say Ganymede, in the litter of the sun;
Say Daphne staeling in the bark, {brook}
Say anyone or say the lark—
Ah, say it was the lark!
Such guile they had, such note
Such inward rolling laud and blat—
Such "Sweet! Sweet!"
As the nightingale had had
His throat cut,
It knaved {harvested} the heart,
Kill'd {slew} absolute.

In 8.1 *Discant (Descant)* and in HON. DB used "Discant" and "Descant" indiscriminately. Not dated; usual name and address in upper right corner. *Pro Vita Sua: Sua* is spelled *Sue.* No. 29 in "List." A third separate stanza beginning "Therefore—Look not upon her horizontally . . ." is crossed out. The last two lines need some explanation (or editing): The original reads: "It knaved her to the heart," with "to" crossed out and "harvested the" written on top of "knaved" without being crossing out. The original typed last line reads: "It kill'd her absolute"; "It" and "her" are clearly crossed out, and "slew" was written on top of "kill'd" without being crossed out.

155

A second copy has some changes: The title is plainly "Descant." The second line of the first stanza starts with "Voyeur" crossed out and replaced by "Procurer." Changes in the penultimate line: "It cored her to the heart"; and in the last line: "Cracked [her] absolute."

The folder 11.2 *"There is no gender . . . ,"* contains twenty pages dated 1967–73. Most of the poems that have the typed first line "There is no gender in a fossils eye" have "gender" crossed out and replaced by "bargain," "heaven," or "sanctuary." One undated copy starts with "There is no bargain in a fossils eye" with "bargain" marked for replacement by "gender, barter, assignation." This folder contains a copy of the poem, dated 21 May 1970, quite similar to this version. The fifteenth line reads: "It knaved her to the heart" with "carved" written on top, without being crossed out. Line 16 reads: "It crazed her absolute" where "crazed" replaces "slew," which is crossed out. Many of these versions have the "canto" format, which is a collage of several different poems containing "Therefore: Look not upon her horizontally . . ." as a third stanza.

Pro Vita Sua: probably a reference to the *Apologia Pro Vita Sua* (1864) of John Henry Cardinal Newman (1801–90). *Phaeton:* son of Helios who attempted to drive the chariot of the sun, which set the earth on fire. *Endymion:* beautiful youth loved by Selene. *Ganymede:* a beautiful youth carried off to Olympus and in general a youth who serves liquors. *Daphne:* a nymph transformed into a laurel tree to protect her against pursuit.

Dereliction (Does the inch-worm . . .)

Does the inch-worm on the Atlas mourn
That last acre its not inched upon?
As does the rascal, when to grass he's toed
Thunder in the basket, mowed to measure;
The four last things begun:
Leviathan
Thrashing on the banks of kingdomcome.

In 8.9 *Approved Poems.* No. 10 in "List." The clean copy has the handwritten "OK" in green ink (by DB) and "German group" in black ink (by HON). There are many different versions in other folders that begin with the same line, for example, 8.10–11 *As Cried,* 8.18–20 *Dereliction,* 10.13–16 *Satires,* 9.19–21 *Laughing Lamentations,* and 11.4 *Tom Fool.* The editors retained DB's orthography for "kingdomcome."

Commentary: Here is classic late Barnes, a poem that is both polished and complete. We see the habitual way that DB in the late poems connects one idea with another. This question is about a rascal being toed to grass. Finally, we read the powerful lines, "The last four things begun: Leviathan / Thrashing on the banks of kingdomcome." What are those last four things, which seem to presage the Apocalypse? The poet is prophet, but she doesn't tell.

The Rounds

Does the inch-worm on the atlas mourn
Some of the seven wonders he's not put in yard?
As old men do, who out to grass are borne
In horned baskets, on a promenade
Of twenty inches. Do they know it? God
Watches them rack their inch of hippodrome,
And with blunt crutches, beat on Kingdom-come.

Lord, what is man that he is in Thy wick?
A cobbled cast of bait, with offset thumb,
Once a jigging boy upon a stick,
Sullen now as a mallet on a tomb.
Where's the purse that was his mother's womb?
(It coined his faces, both sides, good and bad)
Why, round his neck it bangs, for begging bread!

Even so am I, Dan Corbeau {Jackdaw}, Gent
To this carnival of snails consigned.
Out from my city, like a lazar sent,
For being lazy, lewd, costly, kind,—
In that order—on a cold behind;
A wretched bath-chair, confined up in shawls,
Dragging the spaded shadow where it crawls!

In 9.14 *General.* Single clean copy dated 11 March 1965. Handwritten on top of the page: "Not in proper sequence." Example of poetic collage: the first stanza is related to no. 10 (Does the inch-worm . . .); the second stanza is related to no. 18 (Lord, what is man . . .); and the third stanza is unique, as said by Dan Corbeau.

    Commentary: The first line of the previous poem, "Dereliction (Does the inch-worm . . .)," was recycled into "The Rounds," and here the focus is on old men who wonder about the Seven Wonders of the ancient world, but who are no longer ambulatory, who beat on kingdomcome with their crutches. As a specific example, we meet one Dan Corbeau, who, like Dante, is exiled from his city, a kind of Everyman, doomed to be carried about in a bath chair.

Laughing Lamentations (Lord, what is man . . .)

Lord, what is man, that he was once your brag?
A spawling job of flesh with off-set thumb.
Grown so insolent he lifts his leg
Upon the running sessions of his tomb.
And where's the black purse was his mother's bag?
(It coined his faces, both sides, good and ill,)
Why round his neck it bangs for begging bread,
Her Merry thought? The skipjack of the kill.

In 9.20 *Laughing Lamentations.* No. 18 in "List." There are versions with the titles cited by HON in the list, "Alas, how are the rosaries broken down" and "Lord, what is man that Thou art mindful of him?" (*"Life is painful,"* 39). In 9.19–21 *Laughing Lamentations* and 11.4 *Tom Fool,* there are four different poems that start with the same first line. The text used is a clean copy from UMD and two similar clean copies in "Envelope." In the second line "spawling" seems a misspelling, but it is an archaism meaning "to spit with force." *Skipjack:* in the *OED,* an archaism for "fop." See Job 7:17, Ecclesiastes 6:11, Hebrews 2:6.

Commentary: This poem continues the inquiry of the second stanza of "The Rounds": "Lord, what is man?" Here we see a good example of the way in which DB takes the middle section of one poem and polishes it up to make a poem all on its own. (Or perhaps it was the other way around.) The poet asks what man is, then proceeds to answer the question in an exceedingly cynical way. He is "a spawling job of flesh with off-set thumb"; he is insolent, produced by his mother's black purse. Has God actually made this worthless creature in his own image, the poet seems to ask, this "skipjack of the kill," this foppish fellow? Therein lies a great mystery. For DB, God's purposes cannot be known. She continues her inquiry into what is man in "As Cried (Lord, what is man . . .)" and finds even more insults to hurl at God's creature ("Arm-pits hot and rank as crow!"), but comes no nearer unraveling the mystery of just why such a creature should be permitted to live.

As Cried (Lord, what is man . . .)

Lord, what is man that you are famous for him,
And yet more famous that you let him spin?
A flying face, one of the Cherubim
(Arm-pits hot and rank as crow!)
Carl of Lucifer? Or that sorry cheat limb
A dying {crowing} Fable, tooling on a lap,
Without the shins of Mercury, without the feet
Who walked the courtyard of his mother's lap
And "read her up" as woodsmen stalk the tree
And at the top,
Throw the bottom in at Eden's Door.
O loiterer, what woodsman are you waiting for?

In 8.12 *As Cried* dated 22 August 1966. Related to no. 18 in "List."

Imigo

What is he that thou are mindful of him?
how into the parsimony hand of his palm, lays all her face
instructed by disgrace
not eat rapeseed from an antique tongue—
a man too much abused by self esteem,
At the cockshut hour of day,
prone in each others wings they fly—
you must acquire relatives in spirit before you are parented.
The quicksilver of his tongue flickers at zero
the watch of Flora in his hand—
A man too much abused by self-esteem
her grief took the form of ugliness
I've seen old women digging for doll's bones.
Fox-fire, decaying timber—

Related to no. 18 in "List." In 9.14 *General* and "Envelope," the poem has the
Patchin Place address. Not all lines start with capital letters. "Imigo" is prob-
ably "Imago," but the editors hesitated to change the title. In 9.14 *General* there
are two different poems from 1971 bearing the title "Imigo." In *Creatures in an
Alphabet* the poem to the letter "I" is to "the Imago." *Cockshut:* the time when
poultry are shut in for the night.

    Commentary: Although there is little evidence in these poems, one suspects
that during DB's lifetime only her father aroused such anger and contempt
as one finds here. Her rage in *The Antiphon* and even *Ryder* continues through
the late poems. "Imigo" reflects this angry mood, stating "you must acquire
relatives in spirit before you are parented." Then, a few lines later, "A man too
much abused by self-esteem / her grief took the form of ugliness." In con-
versation she repeatedly blamed her family for her lifelong depression. Finally,
this is the most consistent theme in her work.

Dereliction (Augusta said . . .)

Augusta said:
"Had I the foresight of the mole
I'd have taken my paps underground
Papp'd and staked like a coachmans coat.
There suckled darkness, and the goat;
As women must,
Who suckle dust."

In 8.19 *Dereliction.* No. 12 in "List." In the same folder there is a copy dated April 1973 that begins directly with the second line. The original has in the second line "breasts" crossed out and replaced by "paps" and in the third line "buttoned" replaced by "staked."

Commentary: Further confirmation that DB has her family in her gun sights is to be found in this poem, where one finds lines that could have gone into *The Antiphon.* In this family tragedy, Augusta is the mother figure, patterned after DB's mother, Elizabeth Barnes. It is a precise description of the mother's deep sense of frustration with life.

Discant (His mother said . . .)

His mother said
(Who long since in her mother is been hid)
"I am the birth-place and the dead."
"Indeed" he said
"Let it be done;
Let us give our tigers, each one to the other one.

In 8.9 *Approved Poems* and 9.4 *Faber & Faber.* The eight poems included in 9.4 *Faber & Faber* are all clean copies typed by HON, which dates these versions to 1978–80. No. 14 in "List." In *Approved* is a seven-line poem with "OK" written by DB and "UK Group" by HON. In *Faber & Faber* there is written indication with a line to make a single line of the last two, and this is the version used here. There are many related versions in 11.4 *Tom Fool,* 9.19–21 *Laughing Lamentations,* and 10.13–16 *Satires.* In 8.18 *Dereliction* most versions begin with "My mother said," which in later versions is crossed out and replaced by "His mother said," as in the present version. Some versions also include the line "As Cried by DAN." The last line may recall how DB and her mother fought over the past: "Let us give our tigers, each one to the other one."

As Cried (If gold falls sick . . .)

"If gold falls sick, being stung by mercury"
What then, being stung by treason and surprise?
Will turn its other cheek?
And He replies (who is misquoted ere he speak),
"Why She
Who keeps the minerals of Paradise."

In 8.12 *As Cried*, 9.1 *Discant/Descant*, and 11.4 *Tom Fool*. Related to no. 15 in "List." This is a stanza in a long poem or "canto" dated 28 August 1966 and 30 July 1966 (it appears between no. 2 "How should I mourn . . ." and no. 3 "As whales by dolphins . . ." from the list). The first line, "If gold falls sick being stung by mercury," is from John Donne as modified by DB. The original reads: "As gold falls sick being stung with Mercury" (line 345 of *An Anatomy of the World*, "The First Anniversary"). DB uses Coffin's 1952 edition of Donne, page 194. Her copy at UMD is heavily marked in pencil and ink and was bought by DB in 1956. In only one version of the poem (in 10.15 *Satires;* in a group of poems dated 22 March 1968 to 19 April 1968), DB writes "(Donne)" in the margin as the source of the citation. The version in *As Cried* has two handwritten corrections but the original words are not crossed out: "impaled" for "misquoted" in the fourth line and "spills" for "keeps" in the sixth line. To retain the *Conjunctions* text as it was published, we do not indicate the words between braces.

Commentary: The theme here is betrayal, but the larger meaning is elusive.

Who Died That Day at Dannemora?

They say that at the time of electrocution, the victim is made "some other."

"If gold falls sick being stung by mercury"
What then does baser metal do, being stung by death?

If electric fields our plots destroy,
And gravitational decay the key possess;
If fire with flesh can make a new alloy,
And captured lightning pilot that address.
If leaded thongs unbolt "some other" boy,
As smallest moles our hidden cogs undress,
Then ask the jailer warden what he smelt
The day that cinder burnt Van Allen's belt.
What fuel made it resinous, what joy
Leapt through the sonic barrier of guilt?

In 9.14 *General.* No. 15 in "List," where there are four copies titled "If electric fields our plots destroy," "Who Died That Day at Danamora," "Who Was It Died That Day at Alcatraz," and "Laughing Lamentations." Dannemora is the state prison near Plattsburgh, New York. The original has many corrections in ink of various colors and is dated by hand 15 October 1965. The line "They say . . ." is typed at the end of the poem, but an arrow indicates that it should go under the title. As already mentioned, in only one version of the poem in *Laughing Lamentations*, folder 3, does the single Donne line appear with his name in parentheses. Other versions in *General*, folder 2, have a different title: "They say electric shock doth change a man." Others have "Dannemara," "Danamara," or "Danamora." Other versions can be found in the *As Cried*, *Laughing Lamentations*, and *Satires* folders, and most, when dated, are from 1967. In some versions DB uses "Alcatraz" or "St Quentin" instead of Dannemora. The Van Allen Belt (discovered in 1958 by James Van Allen of the University of Iowa) is a radiation belt located approximately four thousand miles from the Earth's surface.

Commentary: The beginning of "As Cried (If gold falls sick . . .)" is incorporated into this poem as one of two epitaphs preceding DB's meditation on the death penalty and, more specifically, use of the electric chair in penal institutions. Though the tone is ironic, DB does effectively capture the horror of the electric chair: "Then ask the jailer warden what he smelt / The day that cinder burnt Van Allen's belt." "If gold fall sick, being stung by Mercury" also appears in "Laughing Lamentations (Laughter under-water . . .)."

The Satirics (They called Jesus . . .)

They called Jesus the holy fowl.
Of love, *Chaucer said:* "the dreadful joy";
Machiavelli: "The wish to be good, undoubtedly
The wish to be destroyed." And David Jones
(Somewhere remarks) "the terrible embroidery"—
But I, Jock one Corbeau, one time a holy fowl,
Now a member of the Parliament of Flies,
Have come to preen opinions of myself?
Why, not at all.
Benedicite! In the posit earth
Out of the vale of Catmose come
Like bees in the snow, out sipping winters thaw,
Sweet Dame my mother, and her sisters (four)
Sipping where their sockets were.

In 10.14 *Satires.* Not in "List." Clip dated 3–4 January 1968, with a general title "The Satirics." The poem is on page 2 of this clip. *Vale of Catmose:* Oakham, England, and surrounding area. The Rutland County Museum in Oakham was erected in 1794–95 on the site of maltings by Sir Gerard Noel Edwards, who lived opposite the museum at Catmose House. DB's mother was from Oakham.

Commentary: In this poem DB begins with five quotations that interest her, but these do not coalesce into any sort of statement. The poem seems to be a draft with diverse ideas that could have been excerpted for other contexts.

As Cried (Sixty years . . .)

Sixty years a foetus and a fool {fowl}
and yet a welcome guest in earth he is,
Still dooling on his thumb in paradise,
Or so they say it is his virtue lives; it is in virtue's rule
I say either place, he sticks to his last, and size
For on the pasture, in the dawn arise
Ladies stark as stones {shoals}
And from the skies falls down, a woman's shoe.

In 8.11–12 *As Cried*. Not in "List." Undated, this poem appears as a stanza in various longer poems or "cantos."

Commentary: This poem is a bit further along as a draft than several predecessors. Just who, precisely, "sixty years a foetus" might be remains a mystery, though one suspects an obscure reference to her father, who, until his mother's death, remained her dependent.

Pharaoh

Pharaohs in stone.
Think on Ramses
No wake wag these:
They sit aloud in silence.
Daughters, wives
Like cleavers slung
Between their knees
Solder of centuries.

In 11.10–12 *Virgin Spring* and "Envelope." No. 37 in "List" ("Think on Ramses no wake wag these," "Pharaoh"). Clean copy with "O.K.," not included in 8.9 *Approved* or 9.25 *Completed* in UMD. Other versions in 10. 13–16 *Satires* and 9.19 *Laughing Lamentations.* Four of the eight lines, with slight changes, are also in the next poem (no. 20 in "List"), "Dereliction (On my spade . . .)."

Commentary: This is a fine short poem that captures the stony silence of statues of pharaohs, a silence that yet speaks volumes about their women: "Daughters, wives / Like cleavers slung / Between their knees / Solder of centuries."

Dereliction (On my spade . . .)

ITEM:

On my spade I'll bring her home,
One hand behind her neck,
One under bum;
Pons Asinorum—
Stiff as adz; a reticence of bone;
And think then on Ramses;
No mane of moss, no lichen on the tongue
To shift their ease.
A reticence in stone.
Sister-wives, like cleavers slung
Between the knees;
No wake wags these.
They solder centuries.

In 8.19 *Dereliction* and "Envelope." No. 20 in "List." Undated clean copies with neither name nor address. *Pons Asinorum:* "bridge of asses."

    Commentary: As mentioned in the previous note, DB's father, Wald Barnes, is the Ramses figure, here threatening to bring his daughter home by humiliating force. Wald kept both his wife and mistress in the one house—thus "sister wives." "On my spade I'll bring her home" is the sort of intimidation one finds directed at Miranda in DB's play *The Antiphon.*

Dereliction (See how the sledded . . .)

ITEM:

See how the sledded tongue reams out of her mouth,
As does the potters thumb reek out his clay.
And as the infant forward falls in play
Upon the kissing or the unkisse'd mouth
Time and the magnet turn him to and fro,
Therefore, how should I mourn, or know
Of that dark bag where faces come and go.

The very kiss that wrankles on the cheeks;
The kiss that festers in the palm,
The maculate and the immaculate
And all who come of harm—
Who fodder in the pasture of her hand
Say
"Every glory rots away!"

In 8.19 *Dereliction*. No. 22 in "List." There are two clean copies in this folder,
one marked by DB with "?" with neither name nor address. There are versions
also in 11.9–11 *Virgin Spring*.

   Commentary: This is a bitter poem that continues the long-enduring mood
of victimization in the late poems. The images do not quite cohere into a
precise statement, but we get the gist from "And all who come of harm— /
Who fodder in the pasture of her hand / Say / 'Every glory rots away!'"
DB had her moment of glory with the publication of *Nightwood*, but now calls
herself "the world's most famous unknown" and cannot quiet the demons of
the past.

Discant (So they went up . . .)

Discant No.

So they went up and down and mainly crying,
Wheeling on their wounds, their looks so fix'd
That no creature nor no man's devising
Not St. Eustace nor his stag with sticks,
Nor Alt Varuna, girding on the waters
Could show why any creature veiled the face,
No countenance being able to present
Why Xerxes whipped the sea
Or what it meant.

In 9.1 *Discant*/*Descant*. No. 24 in "List." Versions also in *Obsequies* (9.27) and *Phantom Spring* (in 10.18 "— *Spring*" folder, i.e., poems with "Spring" in the title). Copy dated "March 25, 1974." *St. Eustace:* a Roman military officer called Placida who converted to Christianity after having a vision of a stag with a crucifix between its antlers; died 118 AD. *Alt Varuna:* in Hinduism, Varuna is the god of the skies and seas; thus, Alt Varuna is used in the sense of "High Varuna."

    Commentary: In this poem one finds three historical or religious references in search of a recognizable theme. Neither they nor others can say why "any creature veiled the face" nor why Xerxes, the king of Persia who invaded Greece in 480 BC, "whipped the sea / Or what it meant." This poem is surely not out of the draft stage.

Dereliction and Virgin Spring (Tell where is . . .)

ITEM:

Tell where is the kissing-crust
Where three labours met; the trine
Father, Son and Ghost?
Not a crumb.
Who broke the bonding of that loaf apart?
Who drank the wine?
Who took the peel
And turn'd the Host on his own heel?
Who made the sign?
Who is the moocher with the down turn'd thumb?
Who capsized Jehova in a ditch
At Gath?
Leviathan
Thrashing on the wharf at kingdomcome?

In 8.18–20 *Dereliction* and 11.9–11 *Virgin Spring*. No. 26 in "List." Other versions appear in 8.10–11 *As Cried*, 9.19–20 *Laughing Lamentations*, and 11.4 *Tom Fool*. Poem no. 16 in "List" is similar except for the first line, "In this season of lost salvation."

   Commentary: In this poem we see the same ending as in "Dereliction (Does the inch-worm . . .)," that is, "Leviathan / Thrashing on the wharf at kingdomcome," the wording having been changed slightly. In the Bible, David was befriended by King Achish at Gath, one of the Philistine cities; in Scarborough, England, there is the annual Gath of Baal, a jousting tournament that would also explain a knight being capsized into a ditch. Here DB has made a poem by compiling, except for line 4, exclusively questions. The poem is a successful attempt to create a sense of power, foreboding, and mystery.

Satires (Or why not ask . . .)

Or why not ask: What of the kissing-crust
Where the great victims {prophets} met. The Trine,
Father, Son and Ghost?
Say what suborning shade, and gulched the wine,
What hand was on the Host. Who keeps the seat?
Someone apart, who fodders on black meat?
Soft you now—
Who licked the vision from the pelvic plate?

In 10.15 *Satires.* Related to no. 26 in "List." Dated 16 August 1966, under a general title of "Lament for Wretches Everyone, as cried by Josquin Coustace and Carl Pasquin and The Mort."

   Commentary: The poem seems to be an earlier version of "Dereliction and Virgin Spring," for one finds "the kissing crust," the Trinity, and other familiar images.

Discant (Pregnant women . . .)

Pregnant women, hard as stone;
Monuments for sheep to lay their foreheads on—
If your ear has a tempered drum
It can hear
The foetus weeping on its thumb;
The grief, fare toiling over bone
And how should I mourn? and yet how should I mourn.

How should I mourn, and yet how should I mourn
Who yet have never been
In any garden closed,
Nor touched the unicorn
His dousing beam—
Nor the trampled lawn
Of some hatched sepulchre have seen
Mary, from the stable of her gown
Ride Jesus in.
                    "Noli me tangere"

Thereafter
Female relatives came shouting roundabout—
"Turn, Son of Man,
Breed back my son—his bone,
The blood and flesh—
The heels and head pull'd on!"

In 9.1 *Discant/Descant.* The poem is found on pages 4 and 5 of a six-page clip dated "September 1970"; clean copy with very few corrections. The second stanza is related to "The Marian Year," no. 2 in "List." The image in the second line reappears in the fifth line of "Dereliction (There are no sessions . . .)." *Noli me tangere* (Lat.): "Don't touch me," from John 20:17, Jesus Christ's admonition of Mary Magdalene.

The Marian Year

How should one mourn who never yet has been
In any trampled list at Umbria? Nor seen
The Unicorn thrust in his dousing beam?
And Mary from the manger of her gown,
Ride Jesus down.

Two copies in 8.9 *Approved Poems* and 9.14 *General.* No. 2 in "List," not with
that title, but quoting the first line, "And should I mourn . . ." Ten versions
in "Envelope." The first one, titled "Epiphany," is dated 10 February 1974 and
is an eight-line poem. Other versions in 8.19 *Dereliction,* 9.17 *Jackdaw,* 9.1 *Dis-
cant/Descant,* and 9.19–21 *Laughing Lamentations.* Some with "Madonna del Parto"
as title. In 11.11 *Virgin Spring* one clean copy has "(Madonna del Parto—Piero
della Francesca—at Monterchi)." A version of this poem from 4 August 1980
in 9.14 *General* is titled "Hortus Conclusis," but it is quite similar to the
Approved Poems version.

Commentary: This is a haunting five-line poem that seems to be a reading
of an Italian Renaissance painting. See Hall, *Dictionary of Subjects,* 316; 327–28
on unicorns and the Virgin Mary. The Piero della Francesca painting in
the Capella del Cimitero in Monterchi (Arezzo) shows the pregnant Virgin
Mary standing in a long blue dress with one hand over her belly, while two
angels at her sides keep curtains open to reveal her. The unicorn is tradi-
tionally a symbol of chastity and purifies whatever its horn touches. It is
also associated with the incarnation of Christ, and here we see a virgin birth,
as "Mary from the manger of her gown, / ride[s] Jesus down." This poem
had an earlier life as the middle stanza of "Discant (Pregnant women . . .),"
which is dated September 1970, four years before the earliest draft of "The
Marian Year."

Satires (The laying on of hands . . .)

(The Laying on of hands being taken off)
There should be gardens in this parliament of flies
And this old fool, as he partakes of time
As his gymnasium—will not survive
Why should he, *grave* with her dread
Mary, in labour with her dream,
Spins Jesus in.

In 10.15 *Satires.* Poem related to no. 31 in "List," found in several pages dated 22 March to 19 April 1968. The last two lines indicate that this poem may antedate "The Marian Year." Cf. "Discant (Pregnant Women . . .)."

Discant (He said to the Don . . .)

He said to the Don, "My Lord
Your dangling man's not crucified
He's gored."
The picador replied:
"Truth is an handled fruit:
Isn't that your finger in His side?"

In 8.9 *Approved Poems* and 9.4 *Faber & Faber.* No. 13 in "List." Both are clean copies. The *Approved Poems* version has the "OK" handwritten by DB and "UK group" written by HON. Different versions in 8.10–11 *As Cried*, 9.1 *Discant*, and 10.13–16 *Satires.* Some versions in *Satires* have "Savillian" (a misspelling of "Sevillan") in the first line instead of "Don"; other versions in 9.13–14 *General* have "Matador."

Commentary: This poem recalls doubting Thomas, who said of the resurrected Christ, "Except I shall see in his hands the print of the nails, and put my finger into the print of the nails, and thrust my hand into his side, I will not believe" (John 20:25, KJV). Here the context is both different and ironic: someone has said that the "dangling man's not crucified / He's gored," which would seem to put Christ into the bullring. Perhaps the spear wound is large enough to suggest the goring of Christ. It is, in fact, the picador who points out that the questioner should know, since it is his finger probing the wound.

Magnificat

CANTICLE

At eight in the morning, when the ladies came,
Turning the rose, the last time, over;
They cried aloud in idleness,
Shouted aloud in idleness,
Asking, in *sanctus Rusticus*, the name
(honour a man slowly)—
Asking
Orgulous, his fame? Was his endeavour?
Who's he, (a stone?).

(Hymns of Virgin Mary,—Luke, I-46–55, as canticle, and beginning)

In 9.25 *Miscellaneous Completed Poems*. No. 4 in "List." In 9:27 *Obsequies* there is a version dated 25 March 1974 with changes in the second verse, where "turning their rings again for the last time" is substituted for "Turning the rose." The phrase "Turning their rings" appears in DB's story "Aller et Retour." *St. Rusticus:* there were four of them. *Orgulous:* perhaps from Shakespeare's prologue to his play *Trolius and Cressida,* in which the Princess Orgulous is mentioned. The name suggests pride.

 Commentary: The Magnificat in the Bible is found in Luke 1:46–55, which DB noted at the bottom of her poem by the same name. According to Luke, the Virgin Mary says, "My soul doth magnify the Lord, and my spirit hath rejoyced in God my Saviour" (KJV). Perhaps this reading marked the beginning of a longer religious poem.

The Great Man

Death and the maid got him in their stall
He's learned to please them now, and speaks no ill
Of that his last "long journey into the night," but as he fell
Hearing the fretful howl of Philomel,
The ark of Daphnis staleing in the leaves,
She cuts a patch, to smarten up his eyes,
And marks the spot for credit, where he fell,
Turning him once and a half about, for Hell.

In 9.25 *Miscellaneous Completed Poems* and "Envelope." No. 9 in "List" with the title "Death and the maid have got him . . ." Clean copy with one handwritten change: In the last line, the original reads "Paradise," which is crossed out and replaced by "Hell." A marginal note has "Eden." In the third line there is perhaps an allusion to the play of a similar name by Eugene O'Neill. *Philomela:* in Greek mythology, Tereus, her sister's husband, raped Philomela and then cut out her tongue to silence her. *Daphnis:* in Greek literary legend, he was a shepherd in love with a naiad.

Commentary: Whoever "The Great Man" is, in the poem by that name, he is surely one with the patriarch of "Pharaoh," suggesting DB's father, here newly dead. "Death and the maid got him in their stall," and the great man is uncomplaining, but as he died he heard the howl of a rape victim, Philomel, with whom the poet may identify. Since his death, he seems to have been in free fall.

Dereliction (For old Rustibus . . .)

ITEM:

For old Rustibus, there should be shaws,
For catch-as-can. Who inward looks
There should be rookeries. For rooks
Who "cover foot" well out of doors
(Who not again their height will make)
There be "coffins" they call "pies"
And here each one the other take
Having no fear of genitives
Nor cuckoos yolks to keep them alive.

In 8.18–20 *Dereliction* and "Envelope." No. 11 in "List." Two copies exist, one clean and the other with corrections. In both copies "genitives" in the eighth line was misspelled "genatives." For "cover foot" see p. 194.

Commentary: This poem continues the satirical vein. "Dereliction" means "willful abuse," and "Rustibus" suggests the Latin *rusticus* and thus "country bumpkin." DB willfully abuses the king of hicks. One reason she often felt contemptuous of Ezra Pound was that he affected an American-rustic style in speech and letters, but one can be surer that the target of her wrath, as in *Ryder* and *The Antiphon,* is her father, who preferred the country life. "Dereliction (There is no sanctuary . . .)" seems little more than a string of ideas that might have been of use in future poems; it seems scarcely even a draft.

Dereliction (There is no sanctuary . . .)

ITEM

There is no sanctuary in a fossil's eye,
Voyeur, pass by.

The slow beat of ladies wings
There should be canyons for such things.
To find something thousand years over,
and of no use whatsoever
What a treasure!
There should be forests for old men to topple in.
Why certainly I've seen a man in tears.
There's breastmilk in his lamentations still
He prowls bereavement like a bitten dog,
And with a banging tail—
Weeps tallow and whiteness prevails
Cries "Abominable!":
The seely merchant with the kiss kill'd hand,
What is that he lend? (For what it lend—
When a man bend
Down in guile to disease
(Purslane, a prostrate plant, growing close by the ground).

In 8.19 *Dereliction.* Related to no. 28 in "List" ("There is no gender in the fossil's eye").

The Honeydew

There is no sanctuary in a fossils eye
Of predators, of parasites and spring.

Up from her coign of banishment
Bound in the rigging of her steep delay
Comes Io {Euridice} on her arm, a field away,
Comes cattle-faced pucelle, a field away,
up from the tackle of her steep delay
waiting on the green, for Orpheus his head,
Bellini's brides, waiting the head of Orpheus
To rise
Sitting out the head of Orpheus
Like to an acre from the earth arising
Comes feisty Io on her arm, a field away.

In 11.2 *There is no gender* and "Envelope." Related to no. 29 in "List." Undated page with some corrections by hand. Two lines (seventh and eighth) do not start with capital letters. In the second line the editors replaced "preditors" with "predators." The third line originally read: "Up from her hours of steep delay," which DB replaced with "Up from her coign of banishment." In the eleventh line, "Orpheus" is spelled "Orphaeus," which the editors corrected. The last line, "Comes feisty Io on here arm, a field away," has "feisty" as a handwritten insertion and "sarcophagus" typed above "her arm," thus offering an alternative last line: "Comes feisty Io on her sarcophagus, a field away." Also, "carries her own sarcophagus" is written by hand on the lower left corner of the page. In the folder there is a different poem also titled "THE HONEYDEW," dated 1 April 1973. *Pucelle:* slattern; a dirty, slovenly person, usually a woman.

   Commentary: The first line of "Dereliction (There is no sanctuary . . .)" begins "There is no sanctuary in a fossils eye." We have seen a form of this line in "Dereliction (Man cannot purge . . .)," which dates from 1971. Now "The Honeydew" (1973) begins with the same line. At other times one sees drafts with "There is no *gender* in the fossil's eye." In any event, "The Honeydew" is a compendium of lines rehearsed repeatedly for some only partially envisioned poem; Io, only dimly glimpsed, finds more promising pasture in the next poem presented here, "Dereliction (When first I saw Io . . .)." Io was seduced by Zeus and turned into a white cow; here she is grazing.

Dereliction (When first I saw Io . . .)

ITEM:

When first I saw Io, she was grazing
That once and sometime dolphin of the bed;
Like to an acre from the earth arising,
Nor not the heavy putty on a coffin lid,
The vast migration in a dead thing's eye
On the pelt {turf} of the sarcophagus she slid
That chief of cattle, wherries in high float
The scape-goat
Onto the sarcophagi
the castrated eye of death looked.

In 8.19 *Dereliction*. Related to no. 41 in "List." Although undated, this poem was probably written before the next one (no. 41 in "List"). Io was seduced by Zeus and transformed into a white cow by Hera. Two instances of crossing out are significant: In the first line, "When first I saw Io," "my dear love" is crossed out, and in the second line, " . . . sometime dolphin of my bed," "my" is crossed out and replaced by "the." In another four-line version (10.16 *Satires*), the first two lines are more explicit: "When first I saw my love, my love was grazing, / That once and sometime darling of my bed." In the sixth line "pelt" and "turf" are omitted. The evolving line of interest is now "the vast migration in a dead things eye." This draft is gathering power and focus, but it is not quite a poem yet.

When First I Saw My Fable

> When first I saw my fable she was grazing
> That one and sometime dolphin {darling} of my bed,
> Who waits to take her chair in vacancy,
> Like to an acre from the earth {sea} arising,
> Heavy putty on a coffin lid
> Slumming in the earth,
> They are in each others mouths and taste of thunder
> Heavy putty on a garden lid—sarcophagus sarcophagi
> Bound in the rigging of her steep delay
> Trussed up, and clambered down with weed {Ivy?}
> Thunder smells of lightning at the root
> As that like iron smells, and iron, blood
> And brotherhood; Hyperion
> Where she lay feigning, on her arms, a field away,
> Up from her coign of banishment
> Bound in the rigging of her steep delay
> Came Chaos, Dark, and night and 10 on her arm

Millepede kind of terrestrial crustacean, especially common wood louse
and armadillo—thousand feet.

In 9.25 *Miscellaneous Completed Poems.* No. 41 in "List." The folder contains two copies that have only "Djuna Barnes" in the upper right corner. One copy has many handwritten corrections.

Commentary: This poem may be an earlier draft of the previous poem. There are some good lines, but no line seems conceptually bound to the next one, except, perhaps, in the poet's imagination. This draft also reflects DB's use of the dictionary for definitions of promising words, which is also a feature of some of her surviving grocery lists as well. She obviously liked "Bound in the rigging of her steep delay," because she uses it twice here.

Discant (There should be gardens . . .)

There should be gardens for old men
To twitter in;
Boscage too, for *Madames,* sports
For memory, poor puff-balls of a day;
Soundless virginals laid on to ply
Suet to eat, and herbs to make them spin
Cuttle and costard on a plate, loud hay
To start the gnat—and then
Mulberry, to re-consider in—
Resign? repent?
Observe the *haute* meander of pavan
But never ask the one-foot snail
Which way you went.

In 9.4 *Faber & Faber* and "Envelope." No. 31 in "List." This is one of the eight clean-copy poems sent 29 October 1970 to Peter du Sautoy at Faber & Faber, typed by HON and marked "UK group." DB made some minor handwritten corrections (the third line replaces "sport and spae" by "sports," and the tenth line adds question marks to "Resign. Repent." Both copies are in the *Faber* folder. Many other versions are to be found in 8.11–12 *As Cried,* 11.3 *There should be gardens . . . ,* and especially in 10.13–16 *Satires.*

Commentary: This is an intriguing poem, and one that DB obviously thought was ready to be shown. Some of the lines can be understood with little trouble, but in the elusive ones there is still fascinating power. The first part of the poem is a list of all the things that "should be," an idea that begins to take a mysterious surrealistic turn with the wish for "loud hay to start the gnat," a very odd priority indeed. There seems to be a running comparison of old men with both birds and animals: they twitter and require suet and cuttle(bone) in their gardens.

There Should Be Gardens

There should be gardens for old men to whimper in,
For where's the great bull-curl that swagged the leg?
Nothing as vanquished as an old man's groin
Where now hangs a sullen bag,
A sac of withered infants on his leg.

There is no swarming in him now,
His heart's an hive
That's banished all its bees,
He keeps alive
By shivering;
Reverberation of oblivion is his motion,
Disintegration now is all as motion;
Yet cat-wise he will fall, all four feet down
On paradise, the upside down.

In 11.3 *There should be gardens*. Related to nos. 30 and 31 in "List." In 10.1 *Phantom Spring* there are longer versions of "There is no swarming . . ."

    Commentary: This poem dates some four years later than the previous one and incorporates most of the title and the first line of that poem, but it explores a single theme: the miserable wretch that is the old man for whom there should be gardens: "There is no swarming in him now, / His heart's an hive / That's banished all its bees." The poem is coherent enough and continues the theme of old men and humiliation.

Satires (The Honeydew)

There should be Fairs for widower and sot;
Stalls for Dan the pardoner;
And for her, whose pang is in her look,
Poor trot—
Silence, in the foot that follows her.

In 10.15 *Satires*. Related to no. 31 in "List." The page has a title "*PASQUINO*" followed by a second line, "The statue on which all travellers depend." The first poem or stanza is "The Honeydew," and the second is untitled and related to several poems, mainly no. 11 in the list.

Commentary: This five-line poem continues the theme of what there should be, but the setting is quite definitely medieval, for we even find a reference to Dan the Pardoner.

Therefore Sisters

Therefore sisters now begin
With time-locked heel
To mourn the vanishing and mewing;
Taboo becomes obscene from too much wooing:
Glory rots, like any other green.

Therefore daughters of the Gwash
Look not for Orpheus the swan
Nor wash
The Traveller his boot
Both are gone.

In 8.9 *Approved Poems.* No. 35 in "List." Typed date 13 August 1974 and marked
"O.K?" by DB. There are three handwritten corrections: In the second line,
"With time-locked heel and chin," "and chin" is crossed out. In the sixth line,
after "Gwash," DB writes "dust" and then crosses it out. In the tenth line, "For
both are gone," DB crosses out "For," but does not indicate a capital letter
for "both" to start the line, which the editors included. "Gwash" is an archaic
Gallicism for "gouache" (*OED*), a method of painting using opaque water-
colors mixed with a preparation of gum.

Commentary: This poem is perhaps destined to become one by which DB
is best known. It sings its lyricism in every line; it is polished and complete.
Yet just who these "daughters of the Gwash" who might look for Orpheus
are, we may never know. "Gwash" is an obsolete form of gouache, a method
of painting, and by this DB could mean a metaphorical reference to women
in the arts. Those who read the poem aloud slowly will derive pleasure from
the solemn, august tone. God has gathered her faithful, and she speaks. This
is the quintessential late Djuna Barnes; here we see precisely what she was
striving for—not clear denotative meaning, but a beauty and brilliance that
challenges us to savor lines that appear to be English, but which still elude
us. "Therefore Sisters . . ." is one of her poetic gems.

Satires (High-society . . .)

High-society, that stately brawl—
Here should be Fairs for gaffers and old wives,
As should be round-about for the ridiculous
Obsequious, who though vanquished, and bowed-down,
Would rise again
When you agree you've been unjust to something lying down
To a wicked creeping man
Who would dismount again,
Even from his mote of dust.
Even an old wasp-head stings
When in death's Bramble you are lost {your sweet man is caught}
in a black patrolling particle—
A spectacle now lost, why think again and clip
The circingle, that has him in its grip.

In 10.14 *Satires*. Not in "List." On a page with other poems, as are most in the *Satires* folders. DB noted "Satires and Lamentations page -19-"and made a few handwritten corrections. *Circingle:* a misspelling of *surcingle*, a girth for a horse or other animal.

    Commentary: The poem begins with a remark about high society but then shows itself to be still in the draft stage by proceeding to disparate subjects, mainly lines about a "wicked creeping man."

Untitled (A Woman Riding Astride)

A woman riding astride came
Riding astride;
A golden ring on her finger fore
Came to the bride's door
To the brides door came a {the} bride
Riding astride.
A cock-sparrow up on the saddle
A cock-sparrow,
An iron padlock, big as a fiddle
Swung at her middle
To save her prayers and her own sorrow and the cock sparrow
And the cock's marrow.

In 9.13 *General.* Not in "List." The title "Run girls, run" is crossed out. "Run girls, run" is the title of a DB story that appeared in *Caravel* (no. 5:1–7) in March 1936; published in Alicante, Spain, *Caravel* was edited by Sidney Salt and Jean Rivers between 1934 and 1936.

Commentary: This poem strains to become a ballad but does not arrive. Perhaps DB was amusing herself with certain poetic effects, but the sexual aspect seems clear.

Satires (*This roaring sea . . .*)

"Freezing cold, and firie heats" (Herrick)

This roaring sea, this ebbing tide,
This mud-martin in my side;
Gift and trespass, love and hate;
Manacle, and unlocked gate.
Entrance dark, and exits end—
Murderer and piping friend—
Love quest, thou art my lodger yet!

In 10.14–15 *Satires*. Not in "List." Undated. Several versions exist; the main differences between this and the other versions are in the second line, where "mud-martin in my side" is either "woman" or "creature burning at my side"; in the sixth line, where "piping" is "darling"; and in the seventh line, where "lodger" is "absence." Robert Herrick (1591–1674); DB's reference is to his poem "Not to Love." *Mud-martin:* probably the same as the house martin, a bird that builds its nest of mud on the sides of houses.

   Commentary: This is a finished poem, one of oppositions: "This roaring sea, this ebbing tide." Amid all the opposing forces cataloged, the speaker says there is a "mud-martin in my side" that seems to link up with the last line, "Love quest, thou art my lodger yet!" There are six rhyming lines, with an awkward seventh, but on the whole it is a poem with clear enough meaning, a certain complexity, and sufficient polish. In prefacing her poem with a line from Robert Herrick's "Not to Love," she makes reference as much to "freezing cold and firie heats" as to the iambic pentameter, four beat to the line form of her predecessor, which she emulates.

Descent (The Coupling)

When riderless a horse is seen
Rearing at the timber line
From a smoking sphincter drop
Braided hay upon the green

Sound a dump for wretched man,
Who in bramble where gripes meet
Is come about to "cover foot"
And to kick his fires out.

There with fingers jack'd and lean
Picks the self from the design,
As down into the wratch and pawl,
Into the bush and shank gone hence
He bear in his turning heel,
To mesh and mortis consequence:
Rarity, and time commence.

In 9.25 *Miscellaneous Completed Poems* and "Envelope." No. 43 in "List." Three copies exist: (1) A clean copy with the title "Descent" and "The Coupling" handwritten by HON, marked "O.K," "Copy -1- (of 3 copies)," and "German group" with fifteen lines, which is the one reproduced in this selection (also in "Envelope"). (2) A copy dated 19 August 1973 titled "The Coupling," with fourteen lines and some differences from version 1 and 3. (3) "The Jacques," undated, nineteen lines (four new lines at the beginning of the poem, then quite similar to version 1, but with twenty-eight handwritten corrections); this version has a typed note on top of the page "(Item from Poems in Passing)." A very clean copy of version 3 is in 9.14 *General* and the first four lines are similar to version 3, but in a slightly different order, and read: "When the ass with wooden shout / Knocks the welkin inside out; / When the wolf on winter's back / Thinks to purge the zodiac." The fifth line of this version is similar to the first line of version 1: it reads "When riderless a war-horse is seen." In 9.4 *Faber and Faber* there is a clean copy, also slightly different, titled "Discant." The main difference is the first line: "When unhorse'd a ghost is seen." The other two changes are "claws" for "gripes" in the sixth line and "raize" for "kick" in the eighth line. In spite of these similarities, this poem appears as no. 44 in the "List." In addition, no. 39 in the "List," "When beasts step backwards from the act . . . ," is a poem related to the others here described, with the first eight lines different from and the remaining fifteen similar to "Descent" (see the note on the next poem). In no. 23 in the "List," "Sing now a land of rank aged men," ("land" is a HON misspelling for "laud" in the poem in 8.18 *Dereliction*), the first two lines are different ("Sing now a laud for rank aged man / Who in the garden where jaws meet"), but the remaining nine are similar to the last nine of "Descent." *Dump:* the word can mean "mournful or plaintive melody" or "to defecate"(*OED*). *Gripe:* "an intermittent spasmodic pain in the bowels" (*American Heritage Dictionary*). *Cover foot:* to defecate (*OED*). See Judges 3:24 (KJV): "They said, Surely he covereth his feet in his summer chamber"; 1 Samuel 24:3 (KJV): "and Saul went in to cover his feet." Cf. p. 181. *Pawl:* a "hinged or pivoted device adapted to fit into the notch of a ratchet wheel to impart forward motion or prevent backward motion" (*American Heritage Dictionary*). Horse and rider seem simultaneously to be defecating; perhaps this is the coupling. Cf. DB's poem "Mule Satires."

Dereliction (When beasts . . .)

When beasts hump backwards for the acts,
The scroll of heaven too retracts.
When leopards claws draw out of sight,
And mice skip smartly from the catch;
When thump-foot kine give up the latch
To lurching calves who tips the teat,
And sitting hens from love go "light,"
And old men come to take the seat;
To lie down in their singular signature—
Upon the timberline,
And pick themselves from the design,
I've seen dogs guarding vacancy,
Even as old men who have no memory—to eat.

In 9.20 *Dereliction*. No. 39 in "List." The version used here has a few corrections and is not in "Envelope." The two "Envelope" versions are from 8.19 *Dereliction* and somewhat different; one is a fourteen-line version with many corrections and the other a twenty-three-line version that also includes other parts of "Descent" (see the previous poem).

Commentary: The poem begins with a promising menagerie doing this and that, then concludes with lines from a previous poem that seem not to further a particular theme. Several of these lines will be recycled into other poems.

Discontent

Truly, when I pause and stop to think
That with an hempen rope I'll spool to bed,
Aware that tears of mourners on the brink
Are merely spindrift of the shaken head,
Then, as the squirrel quarreling his nut,
I with my winter store am in dispute,
For none will burrow in to share my bread.

In 9.25 *Miscellaneous Completed Poems.* No. 38 in "List." Two undated clean copies
with minimal handwritten changes typed by DB. Other versions are in 10.13–16
Satires and in 9.19–21 *Laughing Lamentations.* In both copies "burrough" appears
for "burrow" in the last line.

    Commentary: This is a beautifully original poem, one of the best of the late
poems, and another reflection on death and loneliness.

When the Kissing Flesh Is Gone

When the kissing flesh is gone
And tooth to tooth true lovers lie
Idly snarling, bone to bone,
Will you term that ecstasy?

Nay, but love in chancery.
In the last extremity,
Duelling eternity,
Love lies down in clemency,
Compounding rogue fidelity!

In 8.9 *Approved Poems. Conjunctions* version. No. 42 in "List"; the poem belongs to the *Dereliction* group. One single clean copy marked "O.K." typed by DB. 9.19 *Laughing Lamentations* contains an untitled version (with major differences in the second stanza), but with "Under death's whittle are we all. (Villon)" as an epigraph. In a different version in 8.19 *Dereliction,* the fifth line reads: "No, but in the grip of chancery." *Chancery* in this case is a term from boxing that means holding an opponent's head under one's arm (presently an illegal move). A figurative meaning of the word is to be in a helpless or embarrassing position. In another poem in *Satires,* one finds "His head caught in chancery," clearly a boxing reference, and in DB's notes (box 7 of series III) is the following line: "their heads in chancery (under arm)."

Commentary: Here is another poem that deserves to be anthologized in any volume of American poetry. It is very much in the metaphysical tradition of Donne and Marvell. In Andrew Marvell's "To His Coy Mistress," the speaker reminds his beloved that the grave awaits even lovers: "The grave's a fine and private place, / But none, I think, do there embrace." The gothic tradition of DB's youth is still a strong interest here, but there is a new, tough-minded quality that derives from much thought and very hard work.

Satires (Memory has muscles)

Memory has muscles.
Someone said "No doubt."
"Overhead, liver, guts and gall
Rides in a bird!"
"In a snail," I said, "they creep about."

In 10.14 *Satires.* Not in "List." The poem is included as a stanza in an undated long poem. Clean copy with minor handwritten corrections in the last line.

When I Conjured You

Descant No.

Do not presume I had forsworn the theme
When I conjured you from absence, long ago,
And dreaming of you, that forgot your name,
That you came castled in; nor go
Crawling against the {grain} scheme, nor creep
Into my absence, for a shell,
Nor presume that I assume the mark
Of the chick-tooth, knocking down my wall.

In 9.25 *Miscellaneous Completed Poems,* 10.18 "— *Spring,*" 9.1 *Discant/Descant,* and "Envelope." Not in "List." The single *Miscellaneous* copy is dated 12 September 1975 and has "When I conjoured you," underlined, as the title. In all other versions, DB wrote "conjure" in the poem, and the editors changed the title word accordingly. The "Envelope" version has "Vagrant Spring" typed in the upper left corner and is the text used here. The poem has a numeric indication to move the third "Do not presume I had forsworn the theme" to become the first line. None of the two copies in 10.18 "— *Spring*" or the four copies in 9.1 *Discant/Descant* are identical to "Envelope," based on the marginal annotations, but essentially all are the same poem with minor changes.

Laughing Lamentations of Dan Corbeau

Observe where Corbeau hops, touches his fly
With cold, fastidious alarm, and piping forth
Flora, with the sweet sap-sucking cry
"What, kiss the famine of an old man's mouth!"
The party's "game" as mystery is posed in truth
"High" as a partridge on a peg is "high."
"Rather will I eat my fists in youth!"
So let them go, for God's sake; I'd as lief
She get my wisdom on a shorter tooth,
Nor shall I "eat my other hand for grief."

In 9.19 *Laughing Lamentations*. Not in "List." Clean copy with title, dated March 1966, containing some handwritten corrections. No. 46 in "List" gives as the title a version of the second line, "With what fastidious alarm he fells his fly." "Envelope" has two versions starting with the second line, one from the *Dereliction* folder and one from *Laughing Lamentations*, which is very similar to the one used here, except that the poem is untitled. There are several other versions in the *Dereliction* folders. Since this is a *Conjunctions* copy, the editors note here (but not in the poem) that DB writes "Black Dan" by hand on top of "Dan Corbeau" without crossing out the name.

Commentary: The poem is a satirical poem with some good lines in it, but even more obscurities. Bitter as DB felt about her girlhood, when she was with her brothers they laughed endlessly about the absurd antics of their father, who, for instance, insisted that the children try eating gravel with their food since poultry used it for digestion. Lacking specific evidence, one nevertheless suspects that "laughing lamentations" has much to do with her memories of girlhood, memories that are a mix of the comic and the tragic.

Discant (Nothing's as vanquished . . .)

Nothing's as vanquished as an old man's groin
(Where's the great bull curl that lolled his leg?)
The fruited swingle of his toil, his staid.
The mayfly whistles in the webbing of his loin
And sings it down, as in a minaret
The Muezzin cries the Arab to his drone.
From what part of darkness {absence} are you come?
For what past of darkness were you born?

In 9.1 *Discant.* Not in "List." Two copies with few corrections with "*(Vagrant Spring)*" and "*Descant No.*" typed in the upper left corner of the page. Two versions, dated 3 May 1967 and 4 October 1967, have many handwritten changes, especially in the second and the seventh line. Parts of this poem appear in many poems in other folders.

   Commentary: The poem has lines perhaps recycled into other poems and focuses on the old man's groin, now vanquished by time. This is more likely a poem about a specific old man who haunts her memory.

Satires (Man's member . . .)

Man's member, like the tough swan neck
(Softly lidded as the sleepers eye),
Jewing wattles, swelling in his lap,
And Bang! life has another death between its gums.

In 10.14 *Satires.* Not in "List." This is a four-line poem with many hand-
written corrections about the penis and procreation that express DB's sense
of the absurdity of human reproduction. The penis is swollen to erection,
"And Bang! Life has another death between its gums."

Tom Fool (You have the rough tongue . . .)

You have the rough tongue of the scavenger;
I tell you thus
The skylarks tongue comes down
In time and curries dust;
What value man has—
And Philomel, her butt, tolls in her mouth
"To tell of pain."

In 11.4 *Tom Fool.* Not in "List." Clean copy dated 2 August 1966. For "Philomel" see p. 180.

Tom-Fool (Beware Tom-Fool . . .)

Beware Tom-Fool, who's one uncandled eye,
sees {conceived} all as pregnancy—
By whose testimony should be disbelieved,
A shadow's swallowed by a shadow?
On whose cast of terror were you fed?
"All things cost you love," it said.
"Put money in your glove," I read.

In "Envelope", but not in 11.4 *Tom Fool*. Not in "List." Since in *Tom Fool* and elsewhere, DB writes the name with or without a hyphen, the editors have left the hyphen, which appears thus in both the title and the first line.

Commentary: This is a short, unfinished poem that takes aim at the male figure who sports many names in DB's late poems: Dan Corbeau, Tom Fool, and others.

Jackdaw (When I was an infant . . .)

When I was an infant
Knuckling my foot,
Keeling on the huck-bone,
Blowing through my snout,
It was observed by huntsmen,
(Though they did not shoot)
I was in my *hubris*,
Bowling Gods about.

When I was a young cock,
Rocking on my tail,
Hiking up my cross tabs
And buzzing on the pot,
It was observed by nursemaids
(But my morning wail),
I was gleeing angels,
Were they there or not.

When I was the world's man,
Juggling the plates.
Crouching on the high-wire,
And falsifying notes,
It was observed by counsel
It was among the fates
I should be with Hermes
When rounding on the goats.

But when I was the grave's job,
Slowing in the twist,
Solemn as a thole-pin,
And feathering with care,
It was observed by Yorick,
It's Shylock that he kissed!
Now I am my own man,
Embezzling the air.

In 9.17 *Jackdaw*. Not in "List." Two undated pages (one a carbon copy) with clean copies with minimal changes in the last two lines. No name or address is given. Other very similar copies are in 9.20 *Laughing Lamentations;* one copy has "The Juggler" handwritten as a possible title (spelled "jugler").

Commentary: This is a four-stanza poem with the character of a ballad. There are obscurities, but the poem seems quite complete and rather intriguing; it takes us through the four stages of Jackdaw's life: he is an infant, a young cock, "the world's man," and "the grave's job." As a man, "It was observed by counsel / It was among the fates / I should be with Hermes / When rounding on the goats." This hint that the Tom Fool might sexually abuse goats links this figure to Wendell Ryder, patterned after her father, Wald, of DB's novel *Ryder,* where it is mentioned more than once that Wendell made love to his barnyard animals.

A Victim Is a State of Decline

There's that truth that only victims savour,
When it be young, and raining yet all over,
The crushing of the medlar quince on the tongue
Ruptures the mouth, however—
In some vigil of the earth,
With some greater theme imbued
And some deal later—
But in some spaddle of the earth
And with some subtler theme imbued,
The victor brings the victim, his Mother,
Wrapped in stealth,
Bucked down and whack'd about in slaughter {laughter}
Walking his bones away into himself.

Clean copy dated 1 February 1974 in "Envelope." No. 36 in "List." The edi-
tors could not find an identical copy in the UMD material, which could be
lost or misplaced in the DB nonpoetry papers. A very close version is found
in 8.12 *Dereliction*, dated 24 April 1971, where the two first lines read: "A vic-
tim is a state of decadence / (Said whom?)" and is a stanza in a longer poem
or "canto." In 8.18 *Dereliction* there is another very similar version that forms
part of a "canto" titled "Dereliction, Parthenogenesis and Phantom Spring,"
which contains twelve "items" and the poem is "item 4." In this version also
appears the slaughter/laughter in the twelfth line: the original here has
"laughter" typed and "slaughter" written over but not crossed out. In two
other copies in 8.19–20 *Dereliction*, only "laughter" without correction is given.
There are versions of a closely related poem, "The victim and the victor
stood . . . ," in 11.8 *Viaticum* (see note to next poem) and in 10.18 "— *Spring*"
(two versions in the *Derelict Spring* and one dated 29 May 1972 in the *Scavenger
Spring* groups). A variant of this poem ("The victor brings the victim . . .")
is found in the *Vagrant Spring* group, which appears misplaced in 10.16 *Satires*.
In 9.1 *Discant/Descant* there are versions of both "The victim is a state of deca-
dence . . ." and "The victor brings the victim . . ."

Commentary: The poem bears similarities to other poems by DB and is still
in the draft stage. There are good lines, but one finds repetition and a gen-
eral lack of clarity.

Viaticum (*The victim and the victor stood . . .*)

The victim and the victor stood, straight up to fearfulness and
Or say in some topple of the earth, and later on,
In some desperate qualm of disquietude
All bundled in, and stapled down {sealed} in slaughter
The victor brings the victim wrapped in cloth
Doubled down, and stapled up in slaughter
or say chaptered {castled} in some chapter of the earth
and some deal {after} later
Walking the victim back into itself.

In 11.8 *Viaticum.* Page dated 1 March 1976. The poem is related to no. 36 in "List" (see note to previous poem), which is dated 24 September 1975.

Commentary: This is a later poem that incorporates lines from the previous one, but is hardly more finished. One line, "straight up to fearfulness," is especially interesting because DB remembered it from Josef Pieper. This poem, written some fifteen years after Hammarskjöld's death, may be a celebration of this great Swedish statesman who helped translate DB's play *The Antiphon*, and who died in a plane crash in Africa in 1961. DB was convinced that he was murdered (see Herring, *Djuna*, 288–89).

Ancient Spring (Therefore look not . . .)

Therefore
Look not upon her horizontally
Nor cost her light by lantern-blick
Except her Daimon hold her thrash in state
Expect the phantom wear her ghost for shroud
(She'll wear the feet)
Slay her on the bits, walk her through the rock
And sound the tents and tampons in the brook—
And howl aloud
And lick her hand for its sick with blood
The jump-up jellies of the sheet;
Birdlime of the wood.

In 10.18 "— *Spring.*" The poem is no. 34 in "List." Clean copy on page 5 of
"Ancient Spring" dated 21 October 1973. DB produced earlier versions with
many changes, which are in 9.1 *Descant/Discant* and 8.19 *Dereliction.* The copy in
"Envelope" is from 9.1 *Descant/Discant* and dated September 1970. Undated
versions with changes also appear in 11.9 *Virgin Spring.*

Commentary: This poem appears to portray a woman lying in state, with the
reader playing the role of observer. The poem emphasizes certain realistic
details of death, with blood described as "jump-up jellies of the sheet." Yet
there is a more sinister dimension, for her spirit seems to have been abducted
by a demon or phantom to begin the journey to the underworld, but this is
framed in uncertainty.

Hearsed Up in Oak

Hearsed up in oak, hosted by a tree,
The oyster spreads its mantle on the shore
And ebbs it back again
See how terror ferries forth the tongue;
She walks the horror {Devil}, his tail over her arm.
Man has a rage to be God
A puff of giants in the air, sky
Bulls pizzle dragging gravel.
The French enjoy their teeth
Jobatioh
Dance of the prudish Ladies
Taft holes for asses ears
Charon the doleful hypocrite.
The delicate disaster of his taste
The wine of perfect dress, bantling
Atrocious, but compassionate.
Be careful: "the unhappy are always considered guilty."

In 9.25 *Miscellaneous Completed.* Not in "List." Single clean copy.

    Commentary: The unforgettable title here is classic Barnes, for it captures the macabre and makes it ridiculous. The first line is imaginative and coherent, for to be "hearsed up in oak" is indeed to be "hosted by a tree." After this fine beginning, the images do not much cohere.

Sardonics (Burly ghosts . . .)

Burly ghosts, malevolent and shag,
Come about to rub against his leg;
She swims in his eclipse.
Lucifer, that salmon of the air,
That kiss killing man,
Breeds himself by falling from the air.

In 10.14 *Satires.* Not in "List." This is a stanza of a longer "canto" in a clip
dated 5 November 1968.

    Commentary: This is a six-line poem that imagines "burly ghosts" and Lucifer
in some posthumous state.

Father

If you find him in the weeping mood,
Blind him; if you find him down, shouting to the air
Anoint him; and slay him abroad everywhere.
Think on Chaunticlere and his axed head
Crying elsewhere abroad, everywhere abroad,
A bag {sac} of withered children
On his leg,
Papa!

In "Envelope." Not in "List." Clean copy with "Virgin Spring" written in the
upper left corner and some marginal handwritten notes. No name or address
is given. The editors did not find a similar copy in any poetry folder at UMD.
Chaunticlere: the rooster in Edmund Spenser's *Faerie Queene* (bk. 1, canto 2) and
elsewhere.

Jackdaw

THE EYE BEREAVES

The eye within an eye that has an eye
To see the eyeing eye, all eyes deceive
Who has so tuned the *timbre* of his ears
Hears where Daphnis, goes among the leaves
And hears the leaf fall in the stone
Hears the breaking up of spells
And where Persephone casts up her tongue.

In 9.17 *Jackdaw.* Not in "List." Undated clean page (the dated pages in this folder are from May–June 1965 and September 1969). The title and the last two lines are handwritten.

Dereliction (Over in the meadow . . .)

ITEM:

> "Over in the meadow
> In the sand and sun
> Lived a mother piper
> And her paragon."
> Peep said the mother
> 'I weep' said the one—
> And so on—

∾

Should any note her shag and galled {drill'd} with wear
And ears laid back
Snouted like the cyclamen
Do not oblige with sjambok in the night
Nor let slip the giggling dogs of Africa:
On the weights of night she casts {vomits} hair
(With ears laid back)
And is an owl {a snarl} again, upright.
But from the chin
The beard snagged out
And from the head
The eyes called in.

In 8.19 *Dereliction* and "Envelope." No. 21 in "List" ("Over the meadow, in the sand, in the sun"). sjambok: heavy leather whip.

   Commentary: "Over in the Meadow" is a children's poem by Olive A. Wadsworth, pseudonym of Katherine Floyd Dana (1835–86), containing rhymes about toads, fish, bluebirds, muskrats, etc. DB tried her hand at a verse of her own.

Viaticum (When he came headlong . . .)

When he came headlong through the bloody door
It was his mother freighter that he wore.
The skelit from the skeleton being won {got}
It grew impudent and lifting leg upon
The fawning of his tomb;
The dark placenta, and the bait
Where now the farding-bag and its green swill
The coined his faces with her narrative?
Each the other minting, cheek to cheek,
Each the other weeping back to back?
Who buzzed the vision from the pelvic plate? {plot?}
But soft you now—
At what wharf of Lethe did you wait? {rot}
On what sponge of darkness did you feed?

In "Envelope." Dated 25 August 1974. Other versions appear in 9.26 *Nativity*.
Related to no. 40 in "List." In line 3 the editors have changed "skeliton" to
"skeleton."

  Commentary: DB hated people who parented children whom they could not
support, as her father had done (Herring, *Djuna,* 33), and the poem was writ-
ten in this spirit. *Viaticum:* anything that one might require on a journey. The
invader at the beginning seems more like the Grendel of *Beowulf.* The context
seems sexual, and DB's father did marry her mother, Elizabeth Chappell, and
later take as his mistress Frances "Fanny" Faulkner with the explicit approval
of his mother. The poem is still in the draft stage, but the sentiment is fairly
clear.

Satires

MULE SATIRES

From the green sand, from your cast, take up your life,
The filthy sorrow—
And thy green barrow—
Jack-on-all-fours, Jack-o-clock, poor Tom—
The "figure" of a man who strikes the hours,
And cries
On the outside of the house and woes to the hours.
Certainly I've seen a man in tears.
Seaward and derelict—a desperate man:
And rook'd between him and between
Hay in heaven, and the pasture mares
Whose blown fanned ebon sphincters drop
Sweet braided green upon the scene.

In 10.14 *Satires.* Not in "List." Several copies in a clip dated January 1968 and
3 January 1968. Cf. DB's poem "Descent (The Coupling)."

   Commentary: The poem is still in the draft stage, though there are good
images.

Satires (In some noble show . . .)

In some noble show of root and weed
All the granit Primavera on her stone groin.
Where summer hung—
Takes her by her flint mane, his tongue
Like the potters thumb reams out her mouth,
Sea-pig
To sing his own and plighted song
To sing his journey among drought voyaging
Among sea-groves,
Sea-grapes, and floating weeds and sea codes and heavy as lead
Orpheus—
The strange pard as creep of Africa
The head
This still ounce
Heavy as lead of the Lesbian rule
In her lentitude, drags her toll along
To her charnel in and purrs
In her beatitude, to seek in *sancta rusticitas,* that sacred ignorance
(It is the sea-wreck, saves, swipes the sea,
Think then of that baited bread, the kissing-crust—
Her bate-bird {babe} in her lap
Where three great portents sate—

In 10.14 *Satires.* Not in "List." In a clip of a "canto" dated January 1968 and with the general title of "Satirics."

    Commentary: This seems little more than a collection of phrases that might prove useful in a more focused poem.

Who Does Not Love the Chorister?

(TO MASTER LOUGH SINGING *"Who is Sylvia"* 1933)

Who does not love the chorister?
No budge to be castrated for;
No fiery *chimique* in the balls;
No widow's finger in the curl.
Nor hear the self confessed among the stalls.
Plainsong being his synergy—plain spells.

Pray for him, at the hour of—

In "Envelope" is a copy dated 14 June 1971 with the handwritten note "Mailed to New Yorker June 1971; rejected." No. 47 in "List." Several versions in 8.19 *Dereliction*, also on page 6 of a "Virgin Spring" clip in 8.18 *Dereliction*. The poem is also in "The Cynic Lamentations" clip in 9.19 *Laughing Lamentations*, together with three versions from May 1968 in 10.13 *Satires*.

  Commentary: The poem celebrates the career of Ernest Lough (1911–2000), who was a soloist in London's Temple Church. He inspired a generation of music lovers with his boy-soprano voice. In 1933, when DB notes that he sang "Who Is Silvia?" he would have been twenty-two and a baritone; she was in London during that year and may have heard him. The tone here is certainly ironic, focusing as it does on the boy's genitals (the boy chorister sings soprano without the necessity of castration), but the poem is probably meant to be celebratory.

Satires (Old man cruel . . .)

Old man cruel, with his testers down
Has come to Vichy for his stalking off,—
Watch him race his inch of hippodrome—
With rust fastened, and cactus crown'd
His greatest thought is a cricket, in his skull,
And Nelly, where she lay, like Io on her arm
A field mile away
On the garden of the sarcophagi
What of Hesper, the hump-backed demoiselle, {dwarf, serf-footed}
The calf's foot in the heel, the bell
Of Hesperus
Daemon as well.

In 10.14 *Satires.* Not in "List." On a page marked "-3-" of a "Satirics" clip
dated January 1968.

   Commentary: This poem is another unfinished ode to a cruel old man that
gets lost in its classical allusions.

Dereliction (Hearing the slow beat . . .)

Hearing the slow beat of old ladies wings,
(there should be gardens for such things)
He staggers upright, as one impaired by praise,
(See how deaf the face is!) strange
Nostrils hissing like a blowing {flinching} torch
So dissolute he shuddered in his craft;
Gripping in his water-rising eye aloft
{Aloft} His monocle as he comes about
Hearing the slow bat of old ladies wings
Buggering with clenched teeth

The dog will wag the tail away he says.

Behind the *école militaire*
Squeal upon their fists
The zouaves are biting (on their nails)
See him sprawled upon *espaliere*
He is so licorous and fond of praise
He'd have buggered Icarus, one said
While falling!

In 8.19 *Dereliction.* Not in "List." The second line is related to no. 31 in "List."
Espalier: trellis or framework on which fruit trees, vines, or shrubs are trained
to grow flat.

    Commentary: The humiliation of old men is certainly a familiar theme; it
continues in this poem and the next. Here an image emerges reminiscent of
D. H. Lawrence's famous story "The Prussian Officer," in which the officer
is a sexual predator. The scene in the final stanza is that of a military school.

Laughing Lamentations (When first I practiced . . .)

When first I practiced all my eyes in tears,
With flapping nostrils like a blowing horse,
(O siffleur, too sinful and too jubilant)
Buggering with clenched teeth, his monocle
Girded {gripped} in his water-rising eye, aloft
His little mount from under came away,
Carrying his jock-strap {breach strap} on his thumb
They say if you have a tender ear
You can hear wind go whistling off his back
(So young he'd not yet bitten on his beard)
The heart dies, he said in four minutes by the clock.

Copy in "Envelope" and 9.20 *Laughing Lamentations* dated 26 July 1965. Not in "List." The eighth and ninth lines are handwritten between the lines.

Commentary: This poem is related thematically to the previous one, "Dereliction (Hearing the slow beat . . .)."

Satires (Man does not save himself . . .)

Man does not save himself these days—he's lost the trick,
He bites his beard with inward biting tooth
He is too sinful, and too jubilant—
With "flapping nostrils like a blowing horse"   (Lawrence, D. H.)
He buggers in the latitudes, with clenched teeth,
Song, sung to astonishment, a little dry, tatty turd-knot of a
barrister, who wanted to be *pomander*, waiting on the chill of the
evening, the Grand Seigneur, lying on his slack like a
mastiff, full of rheum, lank water and slow cold, androgynous, senile
optimistic, quell'd with quilted tongue,
intolerable with intimacy and knocking down his nuts,
gimlet eyed. and going under the horizon, lying on Axminster all undone
   and turling twill,

                                                           aghast, his
monocle
Gripped in his water raising eye, aloft.
So dissolute he shuddered in his craft;
"The tail will wag the dog away," he says
And comes abaft.
I've seen an headless cock so stand and stare,
His ax'd head off
As he were crying elsewhere, everywhere.
Skipped her with kisses, like a flying stone
Shied over water (Christ child, when flown).

In 10.14 *Satires*. At the top of a page typed and underlined is "Satires and Lamentations page -19-." Related to the previous poem. After the fifth line the text is written more as prose (without capital letters at the beginning of each line).

Commentary: "D. H. Lawrence" is handwritten in the right margin next to "flapping nostrils like a blowing horse," a line DB also uses in the previous poem. Here we not so much view a rape as read a sermon on man's dissolution, though there is an extended portrait of the buggering man with monocle.

As Cried (She was a creature . . .)

She was a creature given innocence in sin
Weather to wander in, to wither in to dry
To cast skin and tether
Suet to eat, and herbs to make them spin
Caudacity to caulk the sock-shut eye
Decline
Of mummy, mastics, gum-resin bensine
To still the fat feet
Myrrh mingl'd with camphor, knifed in at the belt sheet
Spilth of lex-wax, wild lilt-honey, spelth and salt
Tripped in silence and the cloth; a scale to wear both
Withered, both
One completest silence, the other
Whither on the tooth:
Stealth is both.
Ancient shrines, with spirits bodied
Columns studied, shattered, studded, quiet
(it was found) with tidal dice, loaded.
Ancient splints {cells} with
Ancient cordage careening with cockles in their spiles
to spatch the pitch and hide
The ax handle shivered in the side.

In 8.10–11 *As Cried.* Not in "List." Dated 26 September 1966. DB noted "page 9" at the top of the page. In the seventh line the editors corrected "gum-rezin" to "gum-resin."

   Commentary: DB had her dictionary open to the "sp" section in this poem. She gives us words such as "spilth," "spelth," "splints," "spiles," and "spatch." One has heard of "audacity" but not "caudacity." The subject seems to be a mummified woman, what was found in the grave, and what it all meant.

Laughing Lamentations (Laughter under-water . . .)

Laughter under-water bow'd her head
Like any peasant in a praying stall.
What, do you think to grieve her from the ground,
That somewhat darling of your bed?
If gold fall sick, being stung by mercury
What then the baser metal do
Being stung by dread?
I Dan Corvo, coming home by stealth,
Bend upon myself, my claws drawn,
A bassarid
Claws at the self
Eyeballs on their stalks have long retired,
What does the new-born egg's uncandled eye
Make of this, the new nativity?

In 9.20 *Laughing Lamentations*. Not in "List." This is a stanza in a longer poem on DB's "Page -5-" of a seven-page clip, dated 2 July 1967. The fifth line has the Donne motif from no. 15 in "List." *Bassarid:* in ancient Greece, a name given to those who wore fox skins. In "Atalanta in Calydon," Charles Swinburne (1837–1909) mentions "the Mænad and the Bassarid." See also Canto 79 of *The Cantos of Ezra Pound*.

    Commentary: "Laughing Lamentations (Laughter under-water . . .)," previously commented on, seems to be a collection of images that do not quite cohere.

Dereliction (Cold comfort . . .)

Item:

Cold comfort she had made of it I said,
But think of it, no one is dead
"Tomorrow and tomorrow" but, yet
We hear of it!

Others ask, what is it to be possessed
Of one you cannot keep {slough, shuck}, she being old
There is no robin in the eye to build a nest
For any creature shaking in the cold.
Alcestis?
Someone hooked her to the underworld—
All lovers keep some other feeding Death
Till he get by.

In 8.19 *Dereliction* and "Envelope." There are two undated copies without name or address. The editors used the one marked "?." The first stanza is no. 8 in "List." The second stanza is related to no. 5 in "List" (see notes to the next two poems). The editors changed "Alceste" to "Alcestis" in the fifth line of the second stanza. See also Shakespeare's *Macbeth* 5:5 "To-morrow, and to-morrow, and to-morrow, Creeps in this petty pace from day to day."

    Commentary: This piece is on the verge of being a finished poem, but there are still obscurities to be ironed out. Still, the final two lines are typical late Barnes: "All lovers keep some other feeding Death / Till he get by."

As Cried (And others ask . . .)

And others ask, "What's it to be possessed
Of one you cannot keep, she being old?"
There is no robin in my eye to build a nest
For any bride who shakes against the cold,
Nor is there a claw that would arrest
I keep the hoof from stepping on her breath—
The ravelled clue that dangles crock by a thread,
Who hooked her to the underworld. I said in a breath
I keep a woman, as all do, feeding death.

In 8.12 *As Cried. Conjunctions* version. No. 5 in "List," cited as "And others say . . ."

Commentary: This poem takes the essentials of the previous poem, "Dereliction (Cold comfort . . .)," and blends them together into a much more coherent and powerful statement about possessing, and being possessed by, memories of the dead. The cherished line about feeding death now becomes an effective summary of a deeply felt sentiment: "I keep a woman, as all do, feeding death."

Verse

Should any ask "what it is to be in love
With one you cannot slough, she being young?"
What should it be, we answer, who can prove
The falling of the milk-tooth on the tongue,
Is autumn in the mouth enough.

(The young?)

In 9.25 *Miscellaneous Completed Poems.* The poem is dated 5 February 1978 and is typed. This is a clean copy with "the young?" handwritten at the end of the poem. In HON, page 94, item 25 reads: "Some still ask 'what's it to be in love.' 'The Phantom and the Predator,' 13 July 1973/5 February 1978 (O.K.)." The July 13 date is a mistake because the "Envelope" copy has handwritten "18 July." In *Satires* there are three copies of a long poem (fourteen pages), which includes this poem as a stanza on page 7 without changes. However, the second copy has a handwritten note indicating that it was sent to Peter du Sautoy (of Faber & Faber) on 6 May 1968. In this second copy the poem has an addition (which does not appear in other copies or in the 1978 version): "The young" to the fifth line and a sixth line, "Restore no velvet to the thorn," which explains the handwritten "the young?" added ten years later.

Commentary: This, the last poem in the Collected Poems, is a five-line verse that seems to be ready for publication. Juxtaposed is a question about what it means to love a young person whom one cannot be rid of, against an answer that certainly deserves pondering: "who can prove / The falling of the milk-tooth on the tongue, / Is autumn in the mouth enough."

Notes toward the Memoirs

The selected, miscellaneous notes and drafts by Barnes in the prose section are of interest because they often reveal her creative process in prose and contain her thoughts on T. S. Eliot, James Joyce, the 1920s and 1930s in Paris, and other subjects. None of this material has been published previously.[1]

The Eliot section contains notes culled from many pages in series III, box 7 of the Barnes Collection at the University of Maryland. The various remarks on Eliot are derived from diverse notes and are not to be read as a single narrative, though the temptation may be there. Here there is no sequence to the pages, often no narrative thread to follow on a particular page, and DB's creative process in these notes was probably identical to that of the poems. The numbering of paragraphs indicates units of notes or longer narratives on diverse pages in series III, box 7.

The final section, composed of longer narratives, presents Barnes's memoirs of her Paris days, written in several drafts, with four titles (some or all of them may have been related in Barnes's mind): "Vantage Ground," "A Way of Life," "Farewell Paris," and "War in Paris (1939)"; on one page of "Vantage Ground" the title has become "Vantage Point." Pages are missing, and even had they survived, the drafts might not have been complete. For instance, in the "Farewell Paris" draft, there are two pages with the number 14, and the draft begins on page 2 with Barnes's note that it was written around 1939 in New York. This was not long after she had returned from Paris to escape the war. When these narratives become repetitious, as is the case with DB's memories of Eliot, Cocteau, Joyce, Marie Laurencin, Gertrude Stein, and a few others, the editors have tried to present only her most polished version.

"War in Paris" was also originally written in 1939, though in the years to come it would be revised to some degree. This narrative is an account of her last weeks in Paris during 1939, shortly before the German army reached Paris. At the time, Peggy Guggenheim, who was supporting Barnes, was anxious to see her return to the United States, not only because of the danger, but because Barnes was desperately alcoholic, depressed, and exceedingly unpleasant to her and to other people.[2] This explains Barnes's need for nurses, her distaste for them, and her lack of appreciation for the fact that, in wartime, their services might better have been used elsewhere. Although none of these narratives is polished or complete, the keen observations of Barnes during these years in Paris present a unique perspective on modernist writers and a great city under siege.

Selected Notes on T. S. Eliot

[1] It was Miss Valerie Fletcher (then) who wrote me that it was while "writing me" that Tom got "one of his heart attacks." (!) When, later, I mentioned this to him, he looked surprised and said, "Whom does *she* know, she wasn't there." Obviously she was making it up. [2] Tom said he had "wasted his life" (May 1954). I said, "So have I." He replied, "Yes, but think what you did when you were *not* wasting it!" [3] T. S. E. said that his housekeeper called Hayward the "brains" and he, Tom, the "Saint."[1] (I think he somewhat believes it.) [4] T. S. Eliot said of me, "She is undoubtedly a genius, but impossible." (Abused by praise.) Eliot also said that the last act of *The Antiphon* was the best last act he had ever read."[2] [5] The base Janet Flanner[3] said, "people did not approve" of me, "though I was the best writer in Paris of the twenties," and quoting (out of context), "Djuna says she did not expect me to be as stupid as Tom Eliot about *The Antiphon*." That was to make her of importance . . . I meant that he did not know the story of the play as she did. [6] Tom said (age 69) I'm as spry as a spider!" (Just before going back to marry Valerie). He said, "I never had a dog nor a Noah's Ark as a boy." He said "he'd not, like his grandfather, a beard to keep his neck warm." (This the last lunch, somewhere around January 1962). He said "You've never done anything for me" (this must be because I said I'd think about leaving his letters to me to his wife, Valerie. He had asked me to, through the mail). (He seems to have forgotten a great deal!) On my remarking that Giroux, of Farrar, Straus, and Cudahy, had treated me shamefully, that he was base, etc.[4] Tom said (God knows why), "You like people so long as they are valuable to you, you like people for the advantages you get out of them." His wife was saying, "I'm sure you'll make a very good thing out of the *Selected Works of Djuna Barnes*," which was *not* the point. I said, "Men always like women who make excuses." Tom, to me, "You are putting love on the lowest basis; I'd love her anyway." Me, "if she roared at you?" He, "If she roared, I'd love her," etc.,

which, again was, of course, not the point. The year before, I said that pub-
lishers sent notes to each other that sounded, with their idiotic blandishments
and lies, like love letters. I then remarked that I couldn't see why he was
so delighted with Giroux. Tom: "He's useful." (So? Giroux wouldn't be too
pleased with that.) Giroux gets arrangements made for Tom's lectures. "A
necessity," Giroux says, "as Valerie wants to travel." Obviously Giroux does
not like Valerie, speaks down to her, but not to Tom, naturally. He tried (and
obviously succeeded) in making Tom think I had spoken ill of him (Giroux
knew I'd tell Tom what I thought of him, so he got his distortions in first).
I had said nothing but the same things I'd said to Tom himself, that he'd been
"rather rough" on me regarding *The Antiphon* (held it two and a half years
before printing it), and that he had let me down regarding the New Direc-
tions affair of the offer of six percent on a paperback, which both he and
Giroux had told me not to accept. Not less than ten percent they said, the
price Tom got for his. Tom did deny having said this when New Directions
asked him. I have the notation on this in Tom's handwriting. I told him so.
He said "he'd have to see it before believing it." He is often wicked without
(apparently) knowing it. There are reasons for his "fury" that I can't go into.
November 1965: Valerie said, "Giroux, that pansy, coming to our house, push-
ing his friends on us." (!!!) [7] Tom very conveniently leans on what he says
is his "loss of memory." Someone on 18 January 1952, on reviewing his *The
Sacred Wood* in the *Times Literary Supplement* (first printed in 1920), said that "he
is malicious without knowing it." He has been given better gifts than his
terrors will allow . . .[5] [8] There was dire trouble in the house of Tom and
Hayward when Tom left to get married. Some of it appears to have been on
which one should get a large chair slumped in the seat like a fallen lap. One
fury of Tom's was that Hayward "farmed him out to repay favors done for
Hayward by others." Peter du Sautoy says Tom was as "one demented" just
before marriage, taking care of "legal matters" (I know that he had promised
to pay a year's rent if he left first, and the same for Hayward).[6] His wife—a
great big girl from Lancaster—mouth too small, three-cornered, as if a beak
had been pulled off—flesh too feathery, almost imperceptible eyebrows—will
grow fat. Tom likes her "plump"; she's trying to reduce . . . had "biddy" hero
worship—capable in small matters. [9] Valerie recounted how Hayward
(there's a rancorous and spiteful man!) had Tom in tears, saying he'd never
write another word after the lashing Hayward gave him on his *The Elder States-
man* (which indeed is awful).[7] Talking of it just before he married, Tom told
me that it gave him "shivers down his spine" thinking of it, if he could get
it into the shape he wanted. [10] Of *The Antiphon*, Frank Morley was "more

or less for it."[8] Hayward disliked it, said, however, that there were "splendid lines." Sir Frank Francis, the Director and Principal Librarian of the British Museum, said it was like "an explosion in a nuclear laboratory," and "of the greatest intensity or magnitude." (Tom could not remember who this man was.) . . . Miss Stevie Smith says it is like *The Family Reunion* (she must be a fool).[9] Tom says he does not think so and added "some one of these days they'll say I probably stole it from *you*." Tom said he thought that it might be produced in fifty years. Tom likes my *Nightwood* better, Muir does not, and Dag Hammarskjöld said, while *Nightwood* was a mountain, *The Antiphon* was Himalayan.[10] Tom says my verse "limps," and Miss Smith agrees. The first draft [of *The Antiphon*] was not *intended* to be always regular. Tom's blurb for *The Antiphon* was so malicious and spiteful, though pretending "to forward the book's interest," that I had it killed, but kept the copy among my papers. When I asked him why and how he could write "Miss Barnes has no talent," he squirmed and said he was only quoting *me*! He perhaps referred to my quotation of Isobel Patterson of *The Herald*, who, when writing of my *Ryder*, had said I had "genius and no talent," but what on earth has that got to do with his opinion on the play? He is now given to tittering—he tittered. [11] "What," said Mrs. Eliot, "do you think he (Tom) brought along on our honeymoon to read?" I looked blank. "Tillich's *Systematic Theology*—Volume One."[11] I smiled. She giggled. "But what he did, you'd be surprised." I was so surprised that I did not answer; he was uncomfortable, but beaming, (they footing toe to toe). "He had bronchial trouble the first night." He giggled, saying that he is sorry that he had bronchitis in that sort of voice I do not like (when it is used by Laurence?).[12] [in the right margin in cursive: "His is ? irritable, but there, he tittered!"][13] [in the right margin in cursive: "Wants me to do radio with him. I said 'No.' Wants me to write his Life. I said 'No.'"] They live in Kensington. As for the furnishings, she says that there are pink curtains (God!), gray carpets, and red lights! [O holy] "Red Lights?" I exclaim. She says, "Yes, red, they were there." I mentioned the enormous mirror in 19 Carlyle Mansions (I take it that Mr. Hayward kept most of everything). Valerie whispered, "He was eating Tom up"—very pertinent question. Here I asked Tom how Mr. H was. He said he did not know. He evidently left in the worst odor and got only a few things, a broken chair whose "chest has fallen into its lap" she said, and she brought a mirror, A SMALLER MORE SUITABLE MIRROR. She offered me "a bed in their home." Very kind, perhaps, but I (as usual) screamed, "What! Oh no!" "Why not?" I said, "What a ménage!" [in right margin in cursive: "This about time just after his marriage 1951" and "over"] Later, because Mr. Giroux of Farrar,

Straus & Cudahy wanted it, Tom said that he himself would "father" that quotation from some high official of London Library, that *The Antiphon* is of the "greatest intensity" (or the greatest ?),[14] and I refused it, saying that I would not think of putting T. S. Eliot's name to another man's evaluation of my play. He was, of course, furious. But I was right. [new page] [12] T. S. Eliot, on my looking at him that evening in the gallery where Joyce's effects were on show, and I had not opened my mouth.[15] "What a terrible look!" he said, on passing me, on the way out. "You are, I think, my severest critic underneath." Just before this, he had said to me "I'll smack you in the face before the evening is out!" With what hatred! Because, I think, I had "guyed" him somewhat on being so pompous at the Garrick, where he had taken me to dinner a night or so before. He once said he was "shy" with me. [new page] [13] His wife curries him like a lap dog, his tail over her arm (Eliot's). [14] Autograph hunters swarmed Faber's office, looking for Tom; one felled Miss Fletcher among the ledgers.[16] Max Beerbohm's mistress or was it Wells' [in cursive: "(?)"] left half a bottle of champagne in the washbasin for Tom, whom she called "Poeta."[17] (?) Mrs. Eliot says Hayward was a "monster" about Tom. One day he had Tom, head in hands, groaning, "My God, my God, I'll never write a word again," having raked him sentence by sentence over the coals. Apparently he's saying, ALL OVER London, that Tom was "stingy." Mr. du Sautoy says Tom's preparations for marriage were "wonderful" and extraordinary, with anxiety about lawyers, will, etc., etc. [14] Eliot said that Middleton's *Roaring Girl* was amoral, "becoming moral only by becoming damned" (Faust).[18]

Vantage Ground

[Note: The following page belongs to the "Vantage Ground" narrative, though the title does not appear. Some pages have been lost, presumably the first four, for the narrative begins on the fifth page.]

Gertrude Stein had resided in Paris long before the war. She had seen the contortions of the Cubists, the birth of Futurism, the rising of the Vortacists, and Dada. Back in the days of John Hopkins, Gertrude Stein had wielded the scalpel over the human body; she now waved it over the English dictionary. She delighted in amazing the public; to *épater le bourgeois* was her amusement. She had written *Three Lives* in intelligible English; on that she turned her back with *Tender Buttons*.[1] She sat beneath Picasso's portrait of herself in the rue de Fleurus and told about it all, her stockings rolling about her ankles, a great grave cameo on her great grave bosom, solid and as certain as a rock, [new page; at top: "-6- Vantage Ground"] with a face that was *almost* imperishable. She had been a pioneer in the appreciation of Picasso, and in the music of Schoenberg and Mahler; admitted to a "weakness for Hemingway," and in a lesser degree to gentle malleability of Sherwood Anderson. She surrounded herself with numberless unknown boys who aspired to letters. Chiefly she patronized herself. She would say: "Myself and Henry James."

Some of the Quarter thought her mad, others that she was merely tiresome. Nevertheless, on some few she had a profound influence—Hemingway certainly. If his past works do not cry it aloud, *For Whom the Bell Tolls* does.[2] The hero Jordan of that book says, "A rose is a rose is an onion." Later: "A stone is a Stein is a rock is a boulder is a pebble." If this is not appreciation and a portrait, what is it? Criticism? That word "pebble."

Had France made Gertrude Stein? Well, her brother Leo helped;[3] he had been a foremost critic of painting in the United States, as well as a noted vegetarian. He turned up in Paris, that city of chefs, a vegetarian still and the first to note Picasso. It was well that the Steins were people of means, for both vegetables and Picasso come high in Paris. A Jew is always running both before and behind you, that he may "catch" everything.

Back in 1921 or 1922, Crommelynck's *Le Cocu Magnifique* was the rage of the Boulevards, and Jean Cocteau was beginning to be the talk of the city.[4] Everyone was soon copying Cocteau in what he said, ate, did, and wore. Tough little girls from Poland had the vapors when they knew he was lying pale and quiet in his apartment; tough boys, frail little boys from Tennessee, were trying out opium. Cocteau was as fashionable as a new creation. With the opening of Le Boeuf sur le Toit (the name taken from his play), the Cocteau fever reached its height.[5] He was the *bête noir* of the Dadaists Tristan Tzara, Philippe Soupault, Paul Éluard, Jacques Baron, Robert Desnos, and Louis Aragon,[6] but he was the most positive delight of the young and impressionable, and be it said a few octogenarians.

[new page; at top: "-7- Vantage Ground"][7]

[new page; at top: "-8- Vantage Ground," then in cursive: "*Save*"]

Cocteau was beautiful; he seemed to be made of something more ancient than flesh; [words deleted] a plan in bones as excellent as a Gothic perpendicular; his head might have belonged to Chartres. His hands were famous, long, slender, and aware. Later they lay in white plaster on a cushion of black velvet in an exhibition of his *dessins*. Suave, charming, impeccable, dressed by Chanel, perfumed by Numéro Cinq; shod in antelope; sharp and perfect even to his sharp and perfect eyes he spoke to the chosen few.[8] He said, "I rehabilitate the commonplace." His teeth were very near the skin and the skin very near the skeleton. He said: "*Le café-concert est souvent pur; le théâtre toujours corumpu!*" he set the tragic muse on the circus horse! Fratellini and Hamlet mixed; Greek legend, Christian morality, and the street fair were brought together.[9] In his *Orphée* death came for Eurydice in the black rubber gloves of the surgeon.[10] Horses topped by glaziers were also angels, and Madame Pitoëff walked backward into mirrors with less surprise than Alice in Wonderland.[11] "His conjuring tricks," James Lover said, "so far from making death ridiculous, made conjuring terrible."[12]

He published his experiences under opium, and a goodly number of people who had never seen him took to pipe and pellet; he applauded Poulenc, Milhaud, Stravinsky, Auric, Honegger, and Satie. He was one of the first to speak for Picasso, Dufy, and Braque. He was said to be indirectly responsible for the suicide of a youth that had read *Les Enfants Terribles;* if his heroes killed themselves, then the public would kill themselves.[13] This gave Cocteau an idea, [new page; at top: "-9- Vantage Ground"] his most clever and his most devilish. He let it "get out" that he was about to embrace the Catholic faith, and to take orders. His following, almost to a man, smelling of Numéro Cinq, wearing antelope shoes, dressed by Chanel, flocked to the vow (or so it was said). Cocteau saw them safely in, and then he walked out. He said he had to do something to get rid of them. It did no good. A new group took the place of the hoodwinked; when Cocteau was reported under the weather, numbers of people of all kinds had vapors and lay low. They ran to his piping like the rats to the tune of Hamelin; he was not just a "rage"; he was a malady as deadly as the cholera. He was loved and he was hated; he was never ignored. This was the period of the *Cigale* (the Count de Beaumont was said to be the backer) and the Russian Ballet [Ballet Russe], particularly *Le Sacre du Printemps,* in which an English ballerina (with a Russian name) came into her own on the same stage, I believe, where later the American composer George Antheil was hissed and abused as he sat at one piano of four that should have had performers, but they failed to appear [which brought down a rain of hisses, ripe tomatoes, and opened umbrellas in the audience where Picasso sat, and Joyce and Pound, and everyone that mattered from the countesses and kings to the concierge and the cooks].[14] There were catcalls and bravos. Ezra Pound applauded, but there were those in the audience who raised umbrellas and some in the gallery who threw things. Poiret's insults rang in American women's ears, and his cabaret boat tugged at anchor in the Seine, the mad, giddy after-war hour.[15]

On a day in February 1922, something else happened. Sylvia Beach, an American woman who had a bookshop, Shakespeare and Company, near the Odéon, placed in its window a blue bound copy of James Joyce's *Ulysses;* the earlier serialized chapters appearing in *The Little Review* had been condemned by the summoner and the courts.[16] [in cursive: "(N.Y.)"] [new page; at top: "-10- Vantage Ground"] Expatriate pens stood still. Pernod, Byrrh, Dubonnet, eau du vie, cognac, champagne stood motionless in their glasses as if a great compassless storm engulfed them. This was the man from Dublin, whom they had not seen. They wept in joy and copied in despair. "Father of the interior monologue, I lay down my pen forever; after you a paragraph is an impertinence!"[17] Some even returned home deflated and yet proud, for under the last shirt in the shabbiest suitcases lay copies of the book, banned both in England and the States. James Augustine (he was baptized James Augusta from some confusion in the head of the parish clerk of Rathgar) [(his father was so drunk the day he was christened that once at the font he gave the child a girl's and a boy's name just to be sure)] Joyce was ushering out an age.[18]

Joyce, born in the troubled times of Parnell, educated at Clongowes and Belvedere, Joyce who once had thought seriously of becoming a member of the priesthood, had overnight changed the perspective of all who embraced literature.[19] For well over a decade he made writers in all tongues change tempo. Little Magazines such as *This Quarter, transition,* and Ford's *transatlantic review, The New Review* that Peter Neagoe edited, tore him apart in their pages with love, amazement, horror, and adulation.[20] Portions of *Finnegans Wake* were printed in *transition* under the temporary title of "Work in Progress," and everyone read *The Portrait of the Artist as a Young Man* all over again.[21] His early poems, *Pomes Penyeach,* were put to music by impassioned musicians in dark garrets, and, once in a while, someone was in demand for cocktails, because that someone had caught sight of him on the terrace of Deux-Magots or at the Gypsy Bar.[22] Cocteau's lamp darkened, the moon of Stein went down. [new page; at top: "-11- Vantage Ground"] Joyce was as poor as Job; he lived and had his being in a single room with his wife, Nora, and his daughter, Lucia, (his son, Giorgio, had a room under the rafters) in the rue de l'Université. When his birthday came around, Nora could not get the two things he liked, opopanax, a perfume, or an iron ring for his finger. Nora was as vital, earthy, and biting as he was (mostly) silent. Tall and thin, with an ancient dignity, a flat back head that ran scrupulously into the line of his neck, a patch over one eye, a fine nose, a small, martyred, satirical, and stubborn mouth. There you have Joyce, the Grand Inquisitor come to judge himself and his generation. To question him was to receive a cold, terrible gaze. Joyce alone could question Joyce.

All of this and Paris too. The incomparable Bois, the races at Auteuil, Longchamps, old streets with crazy turnings and lovely courtyards; churches, antiquaries, and landmarks, flowers and perfume, the smell of wine and coffee, of bad French cigarettes and perfect French cooking. All the time was here, your own and every man's. Paris gave everyone permission to get a character. You could take away what you liked and keep it. If you sought smart society, you could know it, if a moldering princess in jewels and laces, you could gain audience (if only briefly). If a great doctor, you could learn from him, a scientist, you could ask him questions, an actress would drive down the Champs-Elysées with you; you could talk to scholars and to statesmen; you could touch the hand of beggars and Rothschilds, or look at the great piano-like tomb of Napoleon and at the unknown, dine at forgotten bistros where chauffeurs cursed each other and fed the sparrows, get wisdom at the Sorbonne, draw at Colorossi's or the Beaux Arts; make an ass of yourself at Ciro's or Yelli's or Bricktop's, dance at Mi-Carême, and get trampled to death at the Quatre Arts, and end up in Les Halles.[23] [new page; at top: "-12- Vantage Point"] You could watch de Castellane spend the Gould millions or trot his little dog; dine at the Pré Catalan or the Château de Madrid; go to the opera or to the *Grand Guignol,* lament the existence of purely tourist-catching night clubs, drink a little too much and find yourself in jail.[24]

You could do as you pleased. The Latin Quarter turned out the best writers; the expatriate made the best citizen. The dreadful thing is not that it was done, but that it is over. [Six dots mark the end of this narrative; at bottom in cursive "See here page 5" is crossed out.]

He said (T. S. Eliot):
I said, "You shouldn't have become a publisher—you should have made chairs or something, for how, in the exigencies of office can you think? (I should have said, "feel;" he would better have understood the limitation.) He said, "I can't think more than three hours a day, and if I'd made chairs, that too would have taken eight hours out of twenty four. I find I work best in such a manner. I keep my activities in parts (movement of hands as portioning time), so many for so many, that's the limitation, feeling is exigent, and requires no less than the forfeit of everything else."
I said: "You wanted to storm Europe?" He said, "That's a quotation from my childish exuberance." "No."
But he did, you know.
[new page; at top, in cursive: "T. S. E.," "Days of *The Antiphon,*" a circled "3," and "May 1957"]
I said to Tom, "Have you pleasant feet?" (Lunch this at 66th Street Long-champs.) He answered, "They are just feet, why?" I said, "Because you have pleasant hands." He walks now as if flatfooted. He has had trouble with his feet, which I did not know when I said this, in crossing him over to where he was staying (Giroux's). Also he walks with toe straight ahead like the Indian. I said it's said to be the correct way. He was pleased with that.

In helping with the manuscript of *The Antiphon* [April 1956], at one point I said, "You must come and sit on the sofa; it has arms and can rest you." He said if he leaned on my shoulder he'd "crush me." He staggered in with the dictionaries, much amused when I asked, like Johnson, why he did not know that word, which was "laced" as in "laced cakes." He replied, "Sheer ignorance, sheer ignorance." Asked what "well-wheeled" meant, and I said, "misprint for 'well-heeled.'" He said (he was nodding), "I should have known it." He objected to my use of *gravitas* and *Burgomeister.* I said, "Dash it, you throw in Latin and Greek; why shouldn't I—you even put your months into the Latin." He only lowered his head. He hates to be jeered. He says his plays, aside from *Murder in the Cathedral,* are better because they are about "people—

real people!"[25] He seemed distraught. Hayward had damned *The Elder States-*
man. I said I'd go. He said he was "spry as a spider," and he arose and left,
to go back to get spectacles left at Longchamps.
Motet sung by Ives Tenier—Giovanni Colonna, fifty years before Bach.[26]
Something in Latin, to God
not force of arms Power? but
The event that has come into its time. Hugo[27]
I said you must in your new play, *The Elder Statesman* (not then finished), knock
the critics' ears off. You know how they now say, "The old eagle sits flapping
his empty vans" etc. He said, "My new play, though it is in the rough, sends
the cold shivers down my spine!" And, he added (angry but controlled),
"You're a scream." I asked him why he hated my play *The Antiphon.* (He had
summed up his feelings with those words.) He denied that he had said it, but
when charged with "fibbing," he said it was possibly "the feline gesture, you
know (arching his arm) the Tiger's Paw, oblique affection." I'm told that he
said, "I'm serious when exhibiting amusement, and jesting when serious."
[new page; at top: "Notes"]
    The bee bustles 'round the bud, carrying summer on the hip.
    Gamers of the pit—cesspit (midden), their heads in Chancery (under arm).
    When I told Edwin Muir that Tom had said he liked my prose better than
my poetry, he cried out, "Oh no!" [TSE] took my (only) fairly comfortable
chair at Cambridge, on May 21, 1957, at the "concert reading" of *The Antiphon,*
and said of my hat, "What's that bandage?" Then he stroked my head and
said, "There's my darling."
    Clout-peg in center of target
    Horseman pigeon—inferior
    He killed cocks and cats, but burned her feather boa, saying it cruel, i.e.,
feathers are cruel.
    Yvette Guilbert said to Henri Toulouse-Lautrec: "You little monster! You've
made me look a horror!"[28]
    Cetewayo that Zulu my grandmother got the (wind car, mouyum?) from.[29]
    The cirrus eye of love and death.
    Do I wink an hooded eye, grow feathers on my chin? Have my elbows on
backward, and scratch my belly of the scale? (If I say "Off with his head!")
That moment my shoulders would wear my hat!
    The lions prize prey? Mice!
    Possibly a vanity to assume that we have been wronged?
    Oh rash impudence! Aeschylus killed by an eagle dropping an oyster on
his bald head, thinking it a stone![30]

Oh don't talk of yourself—all dead (people) have mentioned themselves!
That our affection here may bring her into justice there.

No gross movements anywhere—a quick, delicate dancing step, the hands quartered in midair, check in the touching.

Satisfied with that proper less than all, that beauty of refusal, as Hindus, etc., who will not kiss.

Hands without "appetite" move up the air.

The carpenters' quarters are in the Faubourg du Temple.

corridor rabbit—mating man

Would put you in the pit with Bedlam's Beggars.
[new page]
A still fellow, even his shadow hibernates!

He was a good and reasonable man, and will, no doubt, have a good and reasonable damnation, tempered to his caution.

Shoes from Lobbs, and silks from Liberty's.

At the fountain, (of eternal life, Spa) she was amazed to see those with the most vulgar faces were nearest the cup.

Isadora Duncan (at the last) with her tray-like hat above her baby face, full of roses filled with dust![31]

Do not put too much value on the words of the dying—they also lie.

The swan, that tiger of the lake.

Old ladies with crackling bones. What? Not yet charged with everything? Then you're still unidentified! [in cursive: "eventful"]

She was shocking when vulgar; too small.

The brute incuriosity of the ANGEl'S STARE. Who said this! Tate?[32]

The too accustomed agility in the hands of the *accoucheur.*

A fearful, bland, unhurried man arrived at heavens gate crying, "Pirrip! Pirrip!"

His every gesture approved him.

Any man who speaks in a rich, dark foreign voice makes her think she has a father.

French spring waters, Vichy, Perrier, Vittel, St. Badoit, etc.

Would have been glad to have been lifted and acclaimed.

His cabinet wood, a hard red wood—partridge-wood.

Marcel notes that the lame often wear white gaiters.[33]

Now Freud, to make old men rascals.

My God, what a question: "Did your grandmother try to make love to you?" (Monstrous family questionings.)

The father to daughter: "Have you money to bury the old girl?" (His mother, lying by, in extremis.) "No? Then I wouldn't have asked you to be present."[34]

On the trellis, the cross, the fruit, hanging.

On dead Caesar's lip (the fly), the copulative fly
Performs his office.

Barnaby apprehensive in sleep, and insulting, pushes his fist into grand-mother's face and says, "Smell that!" (sleepwalking).

I have yet to be forgiven for having been abused?

They say the eagle flies with head lower than his heart.

Who is going to straighten the pathetic fallacy that certain of the Milanese, who had the rickets, gave the Christ child figure in bands, to straighten the "Pathetic Fallacy."[35]

[new page] [This page has been detached from its narrative.]

The Vikings on the rue Vavin (Scandinavian).[36] Higher up the Closerie des Lilas, a passion with Ford Madox Ford, and everyone thinking that by going there, they are a long way from the quarter.

The Trianon, facing the Gare Montparnasse, where Joyce was seen every evening dining with his family. And Footit's on the other side, at the Round Point, run by an English clown's widow. There were family portraits on the walls, and it was expensive and chic, because the widow was a clown's woman.

The days Zelli let Flossi Martin eat for nothing if she would sing and bring friends.[37] Bricktop's, Florence's, Grand Écart. Petite Chaumière near the Place Blanche, just below the stairs of the Sacré Coeur, for boys dressed as girls, and for dope. It was often raided. Chez Mon Soeur was also raided often.

The Maldadore on the Blvd. Edgar Quinet had walls decorated in the modern manner depicting all parts of the human anatomy.

The Martinique at the back of the Gare Montparnasse for niggers and whites, white rum their drawing card, drink two and the consumer knew nothing more.

When Lady Duff Twysden, heroine of Hemingway's *The Sun Also Rises*, was famous for always being neat, though she often wondered how herself.[38] She holds the record for waking up in more unknown places than any other woman of the time. [in cursive: "Baroness"] When Mimi Franchetti (—the Rosalba of MacKenzie's *Extraordinary Women*) was[39]

A Way of Life

[at top of page: "3"; The meaning is truncated, perhaps because this page and/or the entire narrative of "A Way of Life" is part of the "War in Paris" narrative. Page 4, however, seems to follow page 3.]
merely bored and unchanged, untouched for good or for evil, but for the hoards of others who would not have been the same, the forgetting is a sorry thing. We are angry with France because she let us down with the fall of the Maginot Line, but she had not let us down for an hundred years.

(The rue Vaugirard longest street in Paris?)

It has become the custom to rail against the Quartier Latin, as against Greenwich Village. If anyone has lived in either or both, they carry a scarlet brand; grudgingly, if at all, the folks back home will say perhaps some of you worked, perhaps one or two were not corrupted by glorias, apéritifs, Amontillado sherry or Rhine wines, cocaine, opium, or Cocteau, and, yes, a good many of you seem to have gotten fame, and a few a trifle of wealth, but all the same. "Ah," you will say, but the Princapessa San Faustino, the American girl who married an Italian prince in her time and came to regret it, in a great bed sitting up in her ear laces and shoulder shawl, she was all right when she went abroad, if only because she never did sit at the Dôme or La Rotonde.[1] And Mrs. Balsan, who was a Vanderbilt and a Marlborough, was alright when she stepped into England, and Miss Beach of Boston, who became the princess of something or other and died eating cake.[2] What of her? Was Boni de Castallani any slur on Anna Gould, her pink palace, and her thousand pairs of stockings? And as a duchess told me, "He gave Anna Gould polish, he taught her the value of time, and he made her international." And did the duel between the Comte de la Rochefoucauld and Henri de la Falaise ruin life for Gloria Swanson?[3] And, on the other side of it, is it to be wondered at that some of the American *demi-monde* have found themselves shipping for South America, Buenos Aires, and Rio de Janeiro as daughters of temptation, or that one of Proust's best friends was an American lad who understood his worth long before, apparently, the Duke de Montesquiou?[4] [new page; at top: "4 A way of life"] For it is a mistake to think of expatriates as sitting always and forever at the Dôme or Le Sélect, tied hand and foot to that spot where the Raspail meets the Montparnasse. The whole of what Paris was got in their blood; you can't eat dinner forever at Stryx, a Swedish restaurant that housed the first American bar, you did not always sit over your *boeuf à la bourguignonne* at Pré au Clercs, the Vikings, the Brown Jug, or at Michaud's. Or take Shrove Tuesday and Mardi Gras and Mi-Carême on the chin forever, sole à la Marguery with its white wine sauce and its overlarding of moules and a bottle of white wine of the vintage years at the Trianon in the company of Joyce with his wife, Nora, and their children, Giorgio and Lucia, who spoke better Italian than English or French, [. . .] grandfather's multi-colored vests and erudition, his thin and sweet voice singing Verdi or the folk songs of Erin.[5] Or Mr. Budgen, who was always trying to claim credit for *Ulysses* and could not bear to be nobody in such close proximity to so much.[6] This had more effect on the young writers of the postwar period than France itself, this man of Dublin who was to set the world ablaze with his new Greek. His literary father, said to be Marcel Proust, was not then nearly as famous as Joyce.[7] Nevertheless one had stopped at Napoleon's Tomb and seen the sarcophagus that looked like a great toneless piano, or had come in from the basilica of Saint Denis, with its royal tombs on which lay the graven images like learned but innocent children, as the crusaders on the floor of the Inner Temple look like bronze fish, beautiful and eternal under the skirts of the sightseers that mill about them. This too the writers of America saw before they again took up their [new page; at top: "A Way of Life -5-"] place on the Latin Quarter terraces amid the cries of the cacao venders and the rug merchants from Africa [. . .] indeed the only perceptible influence that the quarter seems to have had on Edna St. Vincent Millay was the horror of the fact that she bought a goat skin from one of them at his initial quotation.[8] No one has ever let her forget it. The other influence was when her husband, Eugen Boissevain, jumped into the Seine to save a suicide who turned up later as Edna's cook. It is true that Millay translated a few French poems, but they were not a success. Lewis wrote *Dodsworth*, but he might just as well have stayed aboard the boat for its return trip, since France has not changed him, for he did not have France in his blood.[9] Dorothy Thompson, on the other hand, would not be the same had she not spent a good deal of time in Austria and Germany.[10]

In the early exodus, just after the war, not only Mayfair and Peckham Rye, Berlin and Vienna, but Wisconsin and Brooklyn visited the shores of that country, which admittedly had the way of life so perfectly composed that none other has ever approached, far less equaled it.[11] The French carved out an existence that so exactly executed the need of man's soul and body that this has produced the saying that man has two countries, his own and France.

The only writer who comes to my mind as almost entirely deracinated as to subject matter is Kay Boyle.[12] Though her style is that of an American, she has almost never written of her American background. Hemingway [word missing at margin] little, his first stories, *In Our Time,* having been printed in France by Bob McAlmon and his Three Mountain Press.[13] Ford Madox Ford came with his *transatlantic review;* there was the magazine *This Quarter*

[new page; at top: "7"; page 6 missing]
his generation upside down with "J. Alfred Prufrock" and his brilliant criticism, Edmund Wilson, who was always about to go to Normandy, and who loved Edith Wharton's *Ethan Frome,* and the Pré Catalan, and who yet was never anything in manner or apparent liking, but totally American.[14] Alfred J. Knock, who advised someone to look up and document the Nuns' War, or was it Poitiers?[15]

The idiotic things were done, who doubts it? That too many aperitifs, substitutes for the forbidden absinthe, Byrrh, Dubonnet, Calvados, eau de vie, glorias, cognacs, and the old priest of Avon, Gurdjieff armagnac, which will not disturb the soul on its flight toward the moon, Campari and champagne, that there was far too much blind walking and headaches taken care of by the fishes and caviar at Prunières and the Maisonette, and too many strolls on uncertain legs through St. Cloud where one went for mussels.[16] It is true in this life that everything is true, true that too little time was given to writing and too much to feeling, as it now stands . . . did we sense it? We were taking in the last breaths of Rome before the fall, Carthage before the destruction, Pompeii before the ruins. No one in our generation will ever again taste it as it was. Like that now famous madeleine that was dipped in tea, we should bring up its memory with gratitude and love, astonishment and terror, we have walked with Thaïs before she died.

The ham bones of the Couchon d'Or mingle with the bones of our body . . . the loud raucous shoutings of Manhattan's children are not copied by the children who play about the statues in the Luxembourg Gardens, those granite queens who serve as perch for the Paris doves. And the locks of hair, rotting among the violins of the rue Jacob, were cut from the head of courtesans who still ride through the Avenue des Acacias, for the [illegible word], those "debauched artists American" did go to Auteuil sometimes, and sometimes to the fairs [new page; at top: "8 a way of life"] outside the ports, they laughed at the Fratellini brothers, were amused at the evenings at the Comédie Française, awed by Cocteau, the French, and who most influenced a certain strata of both French and America's youth with his doeskin shoes, his impeccable though a bit French clothes (Chanel made men's coats and trousers) his frail, beautiful, meager face, and the legend of Radiguet, the young writer who died in his arms, Cocteau having fed him champagne all night that he might die as he lived, "without knowing it."[17] Cocteau's plays, his books, his final film, Barbette the female impersonator, the only one whose hands did not give him away, had fallen once and was looking for another trade than that of the tightrope and the bar, for a fall to an acrobat is what a full chin is to a beauty, the sign of the coming of the end. There were the Dadaists, later broken asunder by the surrealists at the Cigogne, Camille's, etc., the Princess Murat's elbow in your side at the Dingo Bar as she talked of the beauty of Harlem, Dada, Jacques Baron, André Breton, Philippe Soupault, Tzara, Robert Desnos, Paul Éluard, Pierre de Massot, and talk at the Closerie des Lilas, dancing at the Ball Boullière, Zellis, Ciro's, Bricktop's, Florence's.[18] The Gypsy Bar and its cocottes, the whole of Montmartre as well as the whole of Paris as far as Fontainbleau, and sometimes as far as the Pyrénées, saw the American writers. Some stepped over the border into Italy, and some into Spain, and some landed on the African shores, and all went to Berlin, and some to Chelsea, and some to Bloomsbury, and some on every train and every boat for somewhere, but always they returned to Paris, to listen to the latest innovation in literature or dressmaking, painting as well as foods. Antique shops have changed minds as to periods to love, and books what songs to worship. Some came to translate from the Czech, the German, the Russian, the Polish. Just as in England Arthur Waley was still neck deep in China, so in Paris some unknown aspirant was struggling with Sanskrit (as Eliot did), others trying to learn French, and American French is universally abominable, [new page; at top: "9 a way of life"] Jean de Bosschaire as well as the Count de Lautréamont went to the fore; so did Jean Giraudoux and Rainer Maria Rilke.[19] There were frightful nights and ghastly mornings, there was Guerlain perfume [in cursive: "gorilla"],[20] and there were handsome lace dressing gowns and beautiful overcoats, ties from Sulka's and later scarves from Schiaparelli. Then, again, sometimes in a little street, the rue de la Seine with its old prizes, its Épinales and its *crémeries* and antique shops with china and cufflinks, chairs, fauteuils, and cupids turned the heart over and up from under that stone, the heart, would come a paragraph, a page that otherwise would never have been written.

The plump, prolonged, ecstatic steps of the Wall Street broker's wife dancing with the South American gigolo, who looked over her head into a future that he hoped would be golden, the roulette, the bazaar, the Monte Carlo pavilions, the sea fronts of the south, the promenade at the Battle of Flowers, all of this came back and sat at the Café du Dôme, La Rotonde, Le Sélect, that magnet, the Latin Quarter may have seemed to hold its pins in its teeth forever, but those pins had been drawn from every spot on the globe, and now that the magnet is broken, the pins should not forget.

The terrifying part of it is that it is done. Not what we did, but that it is over.

Farewell Paris

[The first page of this narrative is missing. Many of the notes for it may be found in a list of ideas in a small brown notebook in series I, box 2 in the UMD Barnes Collection. It was probably compiled by Barnes during the 1920s. At top of page: "2 Farewell Paris" and underneath in cursive "Mardi Gras"; also in cursive: "written around 1939 N.Y. (Save for Notes Paris Value [illegible word])"]

Quatre Arts, and how a good many of them borrowed the studio of a lady overlooking the Grande Chaumière to make up on, and how it raised the anger of Parisiennes walking below. How Hiler, the American painter and stage set designer, was one of them with Lynn Holcomb, and the beautiful young girl (dressed as a Roman boy) was another, and how she had to prove she was not before she got in, and how Lynn never did get in and how Hiler did by suddenly seizing a case of champagne that stood by the door and marching forward with it.[1] How no one paid any attention to the friezes of living immorality doing their turn in niches above the dance floor, but how nevertheless it made such an atmosphere of abandon that everyone did whatever came into their heads to do, which was chiefly pouring bottles of champagne over themselves and tearing their costumes off. How they went off the next night perfectly sober, but with terrific hangovers, to see Oscar Wilde's tomb in Père Lachaise.[2] How, the wall being very high, one man managed to drop over onto the other side by the help of the shoulders of the second, only to return an instant later in one unaided leap—somewhere a cuckoo clock had struck.

When Doctor Dan (The Widow) Mahoney (he says its O'Mahoney, pronounced O'Marney) of Kerry-California stock held the entire Latin Quarter in the grip of laughter, the great unpaid, funny, medical man, [new page; at top: "3 Farewell Paris"] drunk every night, yet he claimed to be practicing surgery every morning in some unknown clinic, a student at Madame Curie's.[3] The truths he told and the lies he told made a sort of Venetian rose point of his life. Less is known of him than any one other person in Paris, and he has said the most. He slept in an ermine bed jacket belonging to Mrs. Spreckles; fees sometimes came in the shape of piano throws, oranges, bad paintings, jade beads, and Chinese cigarette holders (from middle-aged women who had him to bridge), and once he rated a stuffed peacock. He said it looked terrible, head down in an ashcan. In 1933, his front teeth were knocked out by an enraged Frenchman who had never seen him before, because he was one more damned foreigner who thought France should pay their war debt. He placed no claim, but had "two bits of crockery" put in. The news reached the front page in New York.

When Marie Laurencin excused herself one fine Monday [in cursive: "Tuesday?"] morning to her beau, saying she wanted to go to the Louvre alone to study primitives, was followed, and when she stepped out of a *bateau mouche* just returning from St. Cloud, she was told with fury that the Louvre was always closed on a Monday. "They opened it for me," she said calmly. She is so nearsighted, almost blind, that she cannot see to paint as others do. "It is my good fortune," she remarks. She carried a pistol until her popularity began to wane, because, she said, thinking of a pistol gives one a certain advantage over other people.[4]

[New page; at top: "4 Farewell Paris"]

When Cocteau was the talk of the town and instigated the Le Boeuf sur le Toit. He even played the drum with his long beautiful hands; people flocked to catch a glimpse of him and his knifelike profile. The place was decorated with his drawings, and his now immortal star and single faceless eyes. Radiguet was the inseparable friend, and scarcely had he become famous for his *Devil in the Flesh*—(he was but a boy then), when he sickened and died.[5] The actors Pitoëff played Radiguet in Cocteau's plays. Young men copied his least gesture; when he wore antelope shoes (very expensive, an effort to keep the mob in its place), young men sold their last finger ring and cloaks of their mothers to secure a pair. When he lay abed and smoked opium, all Paris lay abed and smoked opium. When young children, having read *Les Enfants Terribles*, started to carve themselves up, he took the Catholic vow, spoke of becoming a priest. Consequently, the young men went and became ordained in droves; and when they were all more or less securely locked in the bosom of the order, Cocteau tip-toed out, the only time he lost a whole contingent at one sweep. Chanel is his patroness. He gives exhibitions occasionally, in which, among other things, a Greek head lying on red plush catches the eye; across the place where the heart would be lies a plaster cast of Cocteau's own hand. [in margin in cursive: "Pretty fancy fellow—"]

[New page; at top: "5 Farewell Paris."]
When Gertrude Stein was less famous than her brother Leo, art critic, who has not yet lived down his own line, criticisms turned against him. In writing of some now famous painters' works, he said, "What would Da Vinci think if he were alive today?" He was answered by a brother in trade, "What would Leo Stein think if *he* were alive today." Gertrude used to drive a Ford so small, and she so large, that the quarter used to say, "Here comes everybody." She wore a working man's leather and wool coat, tied her stockings up with tape (they fell down before the third cup of tea), wore a strawberry box for a bonnet; gossiped in a persistent, overbearing, chuckling growl, bought Matisse and Picasso before anyone else, adored young men under twenty-four, then threw them out promptly when they showed signs of maturing, remarking as another went flying down the rue de Fleurus, "He is like the rest, very good company in the summer, but impossible in the winter." She has been the acknowledged influence in Hemingway's life, Anderson's, and a score of others. She speaks of "Myself and Shakespeare" and thinks Henry James about the only English writer. She has a bookcase as big as a Steinway grand piano, bigger, full of unpublished manuscripts. She only writes three or four lines a day, but every day; she says it's enough.

When James Joyce gave up teaching languages in a Berlitz school in Trieste because he knew that otherwise he would never complete *Ulysses*, unless he did. He came to live on the Left Bank with his two children and his incomparable wife, Nora. [New page; at top: "6 Farewell Paris"] They lived in the utmost poverty, yet James Augusta Joyce always paid any and all bills for his guests.[6] He loved to drink far into the night, usually at the Deux-Magots, The Gypsy Bar, or somewhere in the quarter. He would down anis-pernod-suze et fine—[the strongest concoction known to man], a drink that would make any other person in the world completely idiotic for a month, without turning a hair.[7] He loved pointless jokes, studied to be a singer, sings Irish folk songs in a thin mannerly voice, and is frightened to death of thunder (crawls under the bed), of rats (meets them often in the Paris streets), and is superstitious to a degree. He carried the calendar of saints wherever he went, even into the red light district, where he often talked to the madame of the beauty of Greek art, pushing the girls off his knees with the stern reprimand, "*Je suis un prêtre.*"[8] Will not answer questions, likes the perfume known as opopanax, and iron finger rings, and wore red vests that would have pleased any race tout from here to Ireland.[9] Three women have been his luck, Nora, his wife; Sylvia Beach, who printed *Ulysses* (not to count the two American girl editors of the *Little Review*, who printed in that magazine the first chapters before the edition was seized and they went to court); and Harriet Weaver, the English spinstress who gave him her income in the time of his most stress, but who had never even seen him.[10]

[New page; at top: "7 Farewell Paris"]

When Ezra Pound appeared with his red head and beard, smocked in blue velvet, sashed in red, and trousered in workingman's corduroys, he used to appear walking up the Avenue de l'Opéra in broad daylight, carrying a basket full of lobsters, aubergines and fruit pâtés. He lived in many places, near the Seine (the air made his wife ill), and in the rue Jacob. She had to leave, often to Italy, while he remained, writing canto upon canto, and also infuriated letters to little magazines (he was usually the foreign editor) in hick English that made everyone ill. One season he tried to rent out Mary Butts's studio.[11] No one ever went further than the sill. He would nod, pull his beard, and say, "Hélas, it is still working."

"What?"

"Maitland's and Mary's black magic. They used to practice it here. Do you see that faint circle on the floor that they drew the night they sacrificed a mouse? I simply can't let the place; it's got an atmosphere."

When Marcel Duchamps, famous overnight for the canvas at the Armory showing called "Nude Descending the Staircase" (the canvas was ultramodern and looked, as someone said, like an explosion in a shingle factory), gave art up and began carving chess men, chess pieces, and playing chess, and occasionally running down to Monte Carlo with a system (which has not worked yet). He has achieved that miracle, a man famous for nothing. [in cursive: "muck"] [new page; at top: "8n Farewell Paris"] American women would walk miles to see Marcel; if he was said to be sipping a coffee at the Dôme, they flocked. If he was playing a game with Picabia, they hung upon his moves.[12] Finally he had to pretend that he was nowhere just to get a little peace of mind.

When Marsden Hartley and Charles Demuth, the American painters, descended upon the city, and Demuth had to go back home too soon because the change of diet (a very common thing, by the by) made him so sick he could not endure it.[13] When after that, Hartley sat all day long at La Rotonde for fear that he might miss something. Every American does exactly the same thing; they sit for hours as if nailed to their seats waiting on the most famous corner in the world, where the Montparnasse runs into the Raspail, for here the world did pass for ten to fourteen long years, and if one sat long enough everyone went by.

When the Princesses Murat, descendents of Napoleon, amused Americans, one with her erudition, and the other for the way her model told stories on her.

"What! You have nowhere to sleep; I will give you a bed, a very little bed, but a bed. Ah your sister, she is not happy and she is young? She shall sing for me; young girls like so to sing, she will be happy. We will open all the windows, and she can sing so that the cannon in front of the Invalides will hum. Ah yes, so life is difficult. I myself am driven to writing: just a memory, an inherited memory, of Napoleon."

When Glenway Westcott, famous for *The Apple of the Eye*, came by, and the American traveler followed *him* about, [new page; at top: "9 Farewell Paris," in left margin next to "Courbet" is "?painter"] until he became more and more, they say, precious, wearing a long silver neck chain and owning a real Courbet, which only the more exclusive of the expatriates were allowed to view.[14]

When Brancusi, the famous sculptor of what is now called the "batch of eggs," entertained American girls in his great white studio in the Impasse Ronsin.[15] He had one infallible dish, which he called a *cure*, a beefsteak four inches thick, cooked over the embers of his own stove. "When your stomach hurts you, there is nothing like laying it under a pound of beef." He played and sang little tunes from his own country. Everything was white, his hair, his beard, his smock, his walls, his stone, the dust from chipping covered everything with a white powder, and he had a white dog and was happy when you brought him a white flower. The experience was one of peace and heaven the first time; then people (ungrateful world) became tired of the egg sculpture, the stone table, the steaks, the little tunes, the faintly buzzing fiddle. But he played on as the Impasse was falling in.

The days when Harold Stearns, American writer and critic, rather prematurely famous, threw it all up and came to Paris, and how a few years later, drunk and in rags, he told his story, the story that netted him many a dish of bouillabaisse.[16] He was not only following the races at Longchamps, St. Cloud, and Auteuil, but now he had a horse, a racer, a pippin, a winner, if only he could get enough food to feed her. But there she stood, [new page; at top: "10 Farewell Paris"] swaying in her stall, weak for lack of oats. Young women and several hardened men fell for the story about the Harold Stearns horse, giving him funds, which, of course, he drank up.

When Ford Madox Ford started a Bal Musette all of his own in order to finance his magazine *transatlantic review*, and how the quarter talked of nothing for a fortnight but the accident that happened to Mary Reynolds.[17] When Mary went down on the dance floor (she had been dancing with Ford, who is cumbersome), it was the foot of the Baroness Elsa von Freytag Loringhoven that threw her.[18] The baroness, in great distress, knelt beside the unconscious figure as blood was running from Mary Reynolds's nose. Elsa drank what she could not save with her handkerchief, "to honor the blood" that she had accidentally spilled. It was with great difficulty that they got the baroness up from what she thought was Mary's dead body. However, when Mary herself rose up, the baroness was all joy that she had "saved" her life.

It was Mary Reynolds, followed by one man [in cursive: "(or O'Connor?)"; illegible words in left margin, the last one probably "Dan"] and three girls who later saw the baroness's coffin to its grave in Mont Joli Cemetery, after the discovery of the death of the baroness by gas (an accident). The winter of 1927 had been very cold and she had bought an ancient gas stove against the counsel of a friend, because "it looked like a coffee pot." The baroness was German-born, but she had achieved a reputation in America in *The Little Review* and was considered an American; one of the most astonishing figures of early Greenwich Village life. She had a head like a Roman [new page; at top: "11 Farewell Paris"] emperor's, short, sometimes razored, once shellacked, red hair. She batiqued her tailored suits, made earrings from grave-flowers and Christmas tree decorations, and had a voice and a constitution of iron. She kept a skeleton by her bed and did portraits of her past in feathers, paint, and glass beads. She did a "portrait" of Marcel Duchamp, a champagne glass out of which arose tufts of flowing feathers. She was very difficult to know. She thought nothing of breaking your front window with a brick if you would not answer the door, but after you had answered, it was worth it to hear her recite, in beautiful periods, Hamlet and Goethe. She would have been the most sought after woman in Paris had she been wealthy. She knew it, for Paris is a city that makes lions of other nation's *détraqués,* if they can do it in style; she could not.

She was buried in a third-grade (lowest) pine coffin in a hold in Mont Joli, which will be common property in 1937. To our shame, be it noted, we were so grief-stricken that we went to meet the cortège by the wrong gate, and not finding her yet come, we sat at a nearby bistro and drank ourselves fairly blind, going from time to time to the door to see if the hearse had yet appeared. Finally we came to the conclusion that something must be wrong and discovered that we were waiting at the wrong gate. When, therefore, hurrying through the cold fields, we came to the plot, [new page; at top: "12 Farewell Paris"] the earth was already being spaded. Slavinsky, [illegible deleted word] was the only watcher as she descended; he kept the picture gallery financed in some measure by Iris Tree known as the [blank space] Rouge.[19] Of course, Doctor Dan Mahoney said he was there, and perhaps he was; no one remembers now. He tells the story of how he brought a beautiful *corbeille* of orchids and left it standing upright over above the place where her headstone would have been. I recall only five wilted red roses tossed down into the earth and a few posies sent by Allan Ross MacDougall, who, though he loved her, would not attend the baroness's funeral since he had not yet recovered from the funeral of Isadora Duncan. Isadora Duncan, who used to sit about the studios of the Left Bank, fat and drunken, lisping baby talk, wearing a scarlet hat heavy with cotton roses in which there was a film of dust. She was loved by a few and tolerated by the rest because of what she had been. She was broke, yet lived in style at the Hotel Lutétia, while out in the street before its sumptuous doors a dusty broken-down taxi waited for orders. Isadora had hired it in Nice when she had no money for a train ticket. She was unable to pay him off, so he sat and sat.

Harriet Marsland (who admired Isadora Duncan with a passionate devotion) was a dancer who finally gave her one and sole public performance. So frightened she was that she drank a straight quart of rye behind scenes and nearly fell, beautifully, into the orchestra pit. [New page; at top: "13 Farewell Paris"]

Allan Ross MacDougall, a Scotsman, wrote Isadora's life with Irma Duncan and later wrote *The Gourmet's Almanac.*[20] He was probably the only old timer still seen sitting on the sidewalk chairs of the Dôme. He lives gaily on nothing and will not or cannot explain how he has seen the world on less money than it takes to buy a dinner at Ciro's.

He is the deviler of pedestrians, as he sits and sips his café noir, but though he has the tongue of an enraged cheetah, his heart is that of a softy. Almost anyone can borrow from him, and almost everyone has, two francs out of his four.

Natalie Barney, the oldest member of the American colony, is given to Friday teas.[21] Called the Amazon of Rémy de Gourment, her charming and ruined house in the rue Jacob, overlooking a lovely garden, has seen nearly everyone of note in the past thirty years.[22] Plants grow up through the woodwork of the dining room beside the Aubusson. Here have walked Proust, Anatole France, Pierre Louys, Daniel Berthelot, and Rainer Maria Rilke. [in cursive: "TSE.(?) Round"] Apollinaire, Israel Zangwill, Georg Brandes, Colette, Sinclair Lewis, Edna Millay, Carl Van Vechten, the Sitwells, Max Jacob, Lady Rothermere, Lady Colefax, Richard Le Gallienne and his daughter Eva, Strachey, the Duchess of Clermont Tonnerre, Rachilde, Herriot, Paul Morand, Arthur Symonds, André Germain, and scores of others, including Madame Langlin and a Chinese general (female) and models from famous *couturiers.*[23] [New page; at top: "14 Farewell Paris"] Sometimes lady harpists harp, and sometimes Lucie Delarue Mardrus (her husband is a famous scholar and author of the translation of the Egyptian Book of the Dead into French), reciting poetry her own and that of others, sometimes poems by Mina Loy, her "starry eyes aloft," telling Paris what Gertrude Stein is all about.[24] Lucie Delarue Mardrus was the first woman to wear trousers in the little town of Honfleur, but she ran two girls out for appearing in pajamas in the gardens of the private estate of the Duchess of Clermont Tonnerre. She wears a magnificent opal given her by the immortal Sara Bernhardt and now in her declining years has taken to making little dolls and decorated candles.[25]

The night a boy landed from a plane at Le Bourget and said, "My name is Lindberg. Will I have any trouble; I have no passport."[26] How everyone in the cafés was embracing everyone else, even the waiters, such was the happy excitement, how the "boy" was lent a pair of Herriot's trousers, and how every nation was trying to prove Lindberg was of their blood.[27] Konrad Bercovici said that "undoubtedly" Lindberg was Jewish.[28]

When Frank Harris appeared at the Dôme after his troubles with *My Life,* his autobiography, which was banned in every known country, and which he knew had torn down a lifetime of reputation hard earned. He said, as Moore had said before him, "An old man should know when to stop writing; when a man no longer cares to look at a pretty girl's ankles, he should know that he can no longer write."[29]

[New page; at top: "15 Farewell Paris"]

When Aleister Crowley, the black magician from London who had been thrust from that country because he had disturbed the court and half strangled a lady occupant with a disembodied spirit.[30] He was put out of Italy for the scandal of one of his Black Masses, at which a young man had gone mad and died. How he said he wanted to meet Gurdjieff, the Hindu mystic of Avon, with his school in the forests of Fontainebleau, where Lady Rothermere as well as many others went to find out about reincarnation and the moon, "the tomb of man," where, among other things, Gurdjieff teaches one to break down their habits by doing exactly what they can't stand, such as smoking large cigars, drinking eau de vie, and eating pork pie until six in the morning. Here Katherine Mansfield died.[31] He claims that he can cure diseases with a glance of the eye. Crowley never met him as far as I know, but later he met a scarlet-gowned woman, who claimed to be a baroness, whereupon he became the Baron Crowley.

When Bob Chanler went mad and thought that he had a date with every brothel and café, how while at death's door he nevertheless insisted on giving big parties in his studio on the rue Delambre, though he had to sit by an open window trying to catch his breath, for he could neither smoke nor drink and was not supposed to speak.[32] He roared, "On with the party—garçon, champagne?"

[New page; at top: "16 Farewell Paris"]

When Pascin, the famous painter, committed suicide in 1929 (or 30) in his studio in Montmartre, cutting his veins.[33] He had a passion for young girls, mostly colored. He wrote in his own blood on the wall, "Farewell X—je vous adore." His wife, Hermine David (illustrator of Proust), went to the Brasserie Lipp one night with her dog, and when the waiters objected to the dog sitting beside her, she arose and with one gesture swept what must have been a thousand plates crashing to the floor.[34] The gendarmes were called to take her into custody, but Solita Solano, an American journalist, cried out, "You mustn't do that; this is the great artist Hermine David!" "Ah!" said the patron, "in that case . . ." and unmolested David swept out of the café.

When Louise Bryant, widow of Jack Reed, later married to Bullitt, ambassador now to Russia, came to Paris (estranged) and was never seen to eat anything day or night.[35] She said she had an obscure ailment, fat in the blood stream, which meant that she could do nothing but drink. So she drank and at night slept sitting upright in a chair. Now mad, she wears a flying corps blue gray suit and says she is a pilot for the French.

When Adams, a newspaper man who used to talk to Jesus and who said he had killed a man, married a strange woman just because, he said, she claimed to be dead, which was a good idea. How he brought sleep to the girl [sculptress] who had won the Croix de Montparnasse for [new page; at top: "17 Farewell Paris"] staying up fourteen days without rest, by taking her to Père Tranquille in Les Halles and introducing her to "black velvet" (ale and champagne mixed).[36] She awoke two days later to find the bed full of hard-boiled eggs.

When the photographer Man Ray made Kiki famous. Kiki was the most outspoken resident of the Latin Quarter, fighter of policemen, and the amusement of tourists for her ability to show her undies in a perfectly impersonal manner.[37] There was Flossy Martin, the girl who came to sing at Fischer's and who lost her voice on gin. She wore bedroom slippers and thin dresses in the middle of November, because, as she said, "The boys will buy you drinks until you don't know who your mother was, but will they buy you a steak or a flannel petticoat? They will not."

When Anna Wickham, English poetess, married to a professor who gazed at the stars through a telescope until she went crazy, came to town and tried to break up all love matches by saying that she would be big Jesus if the other party would be little Jesus.[38] She drove Natalie Barney to putting her out of her house [illegible word]. Anna had discovered that the sound of tearing paper was the one thing Natalie Barney's nerves would not stand, so she tore up two telephone books and an entire file of the *Nouvelle Review Française* into small bits before Natalie leapt from the couch and had the [new page; at top: "18"] butler thrust her out.

The early days saw every hotel and café raided for cartes d'identités. The early American traveler commuted between Paris and Berlin, for drug-taking was the fashion, and while the streetwalkers and the seamstresses sold "snow" in Paris to eek out their scant earnings, it could be got "over the bar" in Berlin.

Then Gerald Kelly, late of the art gallery Wildenstein, blond, amusing, chic, and penniless, entertained the elite and the low of the entire city.[39] He was the most "called for" man of all. Tea at his house, 44 rue du Bac (the Count de Beaumont's house, which has a reputation all its own) was amusing if nerve-wracking. Endless latchkeys were thrust under his door, as, silently, person after person was refused entrance. Gerald used to cower handsomely in a corner, finger to lip, while his bell rang out battery after battery. Finally he invented, in his mind, at least, an incinerator for "body trouble." It is the only really neat, quick, and soundless method of getting rid of tiresome lovers, he said.

When Jimmy the Bar Man (English ex-prizefighter) laid a now popular radio announcer in the dust with one light upper cut, for annoying the ladies, and how the radio announcer was run out of town because prior to Jimmy's blow, he had knocked two ladies down in front of Le Sélect. His story was that Jimmy had hit him for nothing and had used knuckle-dusters into the bargain. [New page; at top: "19 Farewell Paris"] This announcer, when very drunk, used to break down the doors of the apartments of ladies and try to crawl into bed, where he was not wanted. His story was that he was trying to "clean Paris up of its immorality."

The weekend when Lady Mount ——— of Brittany decided to cement international relations by inviting American youngsters to her château.[40] She planned a ball, a luncheon with the cardinals, and an evening at church.

For the ball she gave the girls permission to dress in her priceless antique costumes. They tore them, spilled cocktails over the laces and satins, fell up the steps, went to sleep in church, insulted the churchman, and as they drove away to the station on Monday morning, flung out of their cars the pottery gifts made at the kiln of Lady Mount ———, which she had kindly pressed upon them at parting.

The days when brawls were nightly affairs, when the *grue* bit off a gentleman's ear and spat it out. How surprised and dismantled he looked.[41] How young girls went riding in the Bois at two in the morning and jumped from moving cabs to be found later weeping in the underbrush. When the Vertige (for women only) opened and closed, the same as Chiappe did for La Fetiche in Montmartre, when private "drags" [new page; at top: "20 Farewell Paris"] were raided, and some of the boys were found to be girls. When everyone went to the Ritz Bar "to recover beautifully," when surrealism was knocking at the ears of Dada, when George Antheil gave his opera for eight pianos and a fog horn, and the riot that followed [which brought down a rain of hisses, ripe tomatoes, and opened umbrellas in the audience where Picasso sat, and Joyce and Pound, and everyone that mattered from the countesses and kings to the concierge and the cooks], one man putting up an umbrella over his head in the pit.[42] When Jacques Baron was the youngest poet in France, and Tristran Tzara managed to keep his monocle in his eye forty-eight hours without once dropping it. When little magazines bloomed and died: *This Quarter, transition, The New Review.* When Titus, husband of Helena Rubenstein the beauty expert, decided to bring out special editions and paid the poets and artists less than they could use.[43] When he thought of having a theatre, and didn't. When Jimmy Light of the Provincetown Players came over on three dollars and stayed for six months.[44] When the photographer Berenice Abbott came over on thirty cents and stayed for years.[45] When Bill Bird (newspaperman) bought a château and found out that it had no water or light, and how he has been sunk ever since trying to pay for improvements.[46] How Gene Tunney appeared one night with Thornton Wilder at the Brasserie Lipp, famous for its beer and frankfurters, and how Alex Small and a flock of other journalists appeared as if by magic.[47] And how Tunney, a formidable just to his lip, had to give up his discussion of literature with *The Bridge of San Luis Rey* in order not to be interviewed [new page; at top: "21 Farewell Paris"], but how he did not get out before Elsie Arden, crooner, turned him scarlet by calling out above the shouting and the tumult, "You can have the large blond gal, dearie" (herself).[48]

When the same Brasserie Lipp refused American clients because the wife of a certain ex–army officer objected when the waiter tried to throw her out, beer undrunk, at closing-hour. Lipp's patron said Americans were impossible drunks, and they were spoiling the place for the French. How the place was shunned for a few days, and how slowly the Americans crept back.

The cave of the Auberge de la Cloche off the Blvd. St. Michel, where the tables were barrels, where an American man, a society photographer, used to bring "his girl," a little French child not more than fifteen, whom he had bought from her mother for fifty francs. He taught her to play the piano, which served her for a living after he left her to return to America and a rich marriage. Later the owners committed suicide for some unknown reason.

Then the body of a girl landing upon it, and hanging dangling, alive above them for some moments before she could be rescued, startled the drinkers under the awning of the Café d'Harcourt. She had jumped from an upper window because a man of the quarter (Blvd. St. Michel) had tried to lay hands on her.

[New page; at top: "22 Farewell Paris"]

La Boule, Place St. Michel, rendezvous of thieves and apaches, though the specialty of the maison was crème de menthe with water. The café at the side of the church of St. Julien-le-Pauvre, where monks met to sing sad and holy tunes.

On the Right Bank there was the famous, dangerous, and therefore alluring rue de Lapp, hangout of the toughs of Paris. The night when Owen Le Gallienne and two girl friends, including Berenice Abbott, got in a roundup, how everyone in the particular café raided were driven to the police station in three black marias; how one girl was stripped to make sure she was a girl; how they were allowed no privacy; how indeed three gendarmes followed the first exclaiming, *"Ah c'est joli, c'est charmant!"*

When the Petite Chaise in the rue de Petite Chaise had the best barman in Paris, the best champagne cocktails, and the best crab soufflé. But how everyone raised their eyes to the little chair suspended over the bar and murmured a prayer for a safe delivery from the place! It was unlucky, it brought trouble, lovers quarreled, and a big shot from Manhattan tried to shoot up the place just to give the owners an idea of how they did things in the States. It finally closed because everyone feared it because it was taboo.

When Michaud's on the rue Jacob at the corner of the rue des Saints Pères was the place to dine, Joyce's choice until later the clientele became almost entirely American. The main dish was Sole Meunière. Once graced with one of the prettiest zincs, it was torn down by the folly of the owner for a modern thing of marble. [New page; at top: "23 Farewell Paris"] How the old man who owned it finally died from snitching drinks on the quiet from his own cellar. How the Café des Deux-Magots, just around the corner on the Blvd. St. Germain, had to be visited at least once because Delacroix and Victor Hugo used to patronize it, but chiefly, if the truth were known, because it has the best, or at least the most American coffee next to Le Fouquet's on the Elysées, and because every other American in the world would be found there.[49] In the last two years the Americans have deserted it for the café next door.

Madame Camille's bar, the Trois As, is frequented by French officers who, with the assistance of something in the drinks, get off with unsuspecting American girls; it is on the rue Tournon, near Foyot's.

The waiter who left the Dôme and built the enormous café and restaurant La Coupole right next door, as large as the Grand Central Station, and how it was a success, though nobody believed it could be.

The old Dingo Bar on the rue Delambre, started by Old Man Dingo, Man Ray, and Kiki, as a place for intellectuals only, how they tried to keep it exclusive and how they failed. Old Man Dingo was ruined by giving credit to broke artists and writers. Later Mr. and Mrs. Wilson bought it; it is now the most depressing of the quarter and brews more trouble. Old Stryx, Swedish fellow, went out of business because the hors d'oeuvres were suspect, [new page; at top "24 Farewell Paris," below in cursive "Franchetti"] demoralizing the waiters by giving fifty or a hundred franc tips for fifty francs consummation. When a certain American clothes boiler manufacturer's daughter (Martha) managed to marry a marquis because his family despaired of his ever becoming a father, and because they thought (erroneously) that she was rich, tried to get off with the family jewels when she saw a separation or a divorce or an annulment in the offing (she refused to have children), and how the French aristocrat was too much for her. He locked her out the very night she thought of decamping. She still uses the title marquise, though she has no right to it. It goes very strong in the Middle West.

When Michael Romanoff came and went, when expatriate Frenchmen used to come to Paris to meet American girls, when Edna Millay's husband jumped into the Seine to save a drowning woman (no Frenchman moved to do so) and they had to keep her as a cook.[50] When life was charming and inexpensive, and every corner a new adventure; the old shops, the old signs, the antiquaries, the kiosks, the sound of the French cab horns, the subway like a doll's train, the funny advertisements, chiefly ugly, the theaters (very bad), the music halls (usually worse), the historic spots, the places you did not dare to visit, the walls of Paris, and visited. [New page; at top in cursive: "25 Farewell Paris"] The blood-chilling stories of chauffeurs who drove you outside of Paris and held you up, and how it came true. The processions of officers with horses' tails in their helmets on high-stepping horses with their own tails. Jazz players who couldn't play jazz, American dancing done all wrong, the terrible French radio, the worse concierges. The tipping at every turn, the time a fish vender from Les Halles tore your clothes half off because she hated the English and thought you were English. When a *chômeur* in the subway tried to trip you up three times because he thought you were American and you

were, and not only that, but a mad one about to swing on him when a gentle-
man stepped forward and said in broken English, "Don't do that, you cannot
hit a Frenchman for anything, you must call the police, or if you do hit a
Frenchman, there are only two places that are legal, the other one is the side
of the neck." And one million other things, and stories.

[New page; note that this page, with "14 Farewell Paris" at the top, represents
a different, perhaps earlier draft, than the one presented earlier. Although it
is page 14, it is not from this draft, which contains its own page 14.] When
the Dôme waiters had to put in half an hour extra every night after closing
to clean off the dirty pictures drawn by Kisling.[51] Old Karus, a familiar figure,
a man who spoke a dozen tongues perfectly and without accent, and who was
followed by a mangy dog, upset the quarter by leaving fleas all over the *trot-
toir*. When Hiler and Wyn Holcomb wore beards and capes and when Hiler's
mistress stole the cash register from Le Jockey, at which Hiler played the piano
(as well as owned the joint), and he said it wasn't the money she took that
he minded, if only she had not stolen his trousers and pet parrot.

When the students all made up on a balcony overlooking the Grand
Chaumière to the horror of the public, greasing for the near nude ball, the
Quatre Arts, into which people often did not gain access. Hiler got in by
seizing a case of champagne. The young woman with him dressed as a Roman
boy had to prove she was an American girl. The frieze of unmentionable activ-
ities gave the place an atmosphere that was "irreplaceable." Curtained booths
served drinks, and here the young Roman girl was sitting imbibing her tenth
pernod when someone, seeing her feet stick out, seized them and dragged her
the length of [end of narrative]

War in Paris
(1939)

[There are two versions of this document. At the top of one copy of the first page is "War in Paris," DB's name and address, and "about 1939–40." At the top of the other first page is her name and address, and "(Save for notes—otherwise worthless.)" The date in parentheses next to the title is DB's.]

It started with a high fever, and it ended with a war. Through the fever and through the war, I learned about nurses and doctors and hospitals and friends and acquaintances and little people in trouble that I had never thought to know; I learned of that slow disqualification that pride and dignity suffer when one fights to live through impersonal and personal attack.

The first nurse sent to me was an old French woman who looked as if she were afraid that no one would be ill soon enough to pay her rent. She carried an antique medical bag, out of which she took dusty cotton, an evil-looking pair of medical scissors, and a hypodermic. She muttered and accused God for her condition (I was to discover that a great number of nurses come to you to tell you their troubles and to be waited on); it was grievous, wasn't it, that she, who had helped so many in and out of this world, should be brought so low that she had to come to her age without a nurse's proper cape? In a feeble voice I inquired how much a proper cape would be. About a hundred francs. I gave her the hundred francs and when she had gone told the hotel not to let her in again.

The second can only be described by saying that she suddenly blossomed in the room. She was full-bosomed and bright of eye and black of hair. She was painted, perfumed, brisk, and delighted to live and to push a needle into you as if she were mending a harness. She leaned slightly back when she spoke, and she spoke of her husband, whose grave she passed every twenty-four hours. She said she had treated him right, dead and alive; he had liked everything that was bad for him, and she had seen to it that he got it. That same day I moved to another hotel; I decided that this doctor and his nurses were not the thing for me. There was also another reason; in the middle of the night I had had to fight the *garçon*, who was sprawling lightly over the bed in an attempt to get my purse.

I went to the American Hospital, on the twenty-ninth of August, I had been too ill for too long to care about the news and the newspapers; I had not the faintest idea that all of France was expecting a declaration of war, and I am afraid that at that moment I did not care, I might have guessed it, however, as I got almost no attention at all. I was put to bed, given a *sédatif*, and promptly forgotten. I rang the bell, a blue light appeared above the door and remained there, no nurse came, no intern, no doctor, nothing. I had to get up myself and look about for a glass and get a drink from the tap outside. In the three days I was there I got fed, and I got three little brown pills and one nurse who would come if you rang for her. It was she who tried to pacify me (for I was having a nervous breakdown even if they did not know it). The screaming that I was objecting to was impossible to prevent; it was a madame in childbed. The dogs I heard snarling and barking all night were those of a neighbor and could not be killed; the sounds along the corridor, as of a thousand dish-pans being kicked over by a horse, were only a mishap with an hundred weight of ice for the gentleman next door, who was under an oxygen tent and had to have it, and, as unfortunately it had landed at my door, they had decided to chop it up where it was, as the gentleman was in a hurry. Then drawing the curtains, she said, "Tonight we may get it; in any case, tomorrow we evacuate for Etretat."

As I had been so entirely forgotten as it was, I decided that I was not going to Etretat, but back to my hotel. I was furious when I crawled down into the lobby to see so many doctors in one place. The nurse admitted that they had all been so interested in what was going to happen to them, where they were to be stationed, and what they should do if the hospital were to be flooded with the wounded, that just ordinary sicknesses like breakdowns and gentlemen dying under oxygen tents meant little or nothing.

It was my first taste of the "war of nerves" in France. I had gone through it the year before in England, and here it was again. A taxi? There were few (all the young drivers had been called). Busses? Only once now and again and only on certain routes. A subway? Only on detailed lines. To walk, well, one could always walk if their legs could hold them, but mine could not. I sat and waited. By good luck a taxi did come, and I gave the address of the Hotel Récamier only to find it empty, with a great chain and padlock hanging under the handle. Inside were some of my things, and there they will be until . . .

Now, through the mists of pneumonia, which had set in, I began to know nurses and war. The few people I knew, who had bragged that under no circumstances would they leave Paris in the case of war, had fled in all directions; the one or two acquaintances left were tired of my being ill, my finances were almost nowhere, and I was lying in the dusty, old, small hotel that I had lived in when I had first come to Paris some seventeen years before, the Hotel Académie. No one was left to run it but a very old man and a very old woman. I came back to it through a Paris that I had once lived in for fifteen years, and now it stood before me like a friend who had no memory.

I thought, man can have everything, but he can keep nothing. When Christ said that man must give up his worldly possessions to follow him he stated a fact. Man is now yet more desolate, for he must lose his possessions and his life with his convictions shaken.

At night Paris was an inverted sky, even darker than the night, trawled by the cabled net with its faint silver balloons. The blackout was so complete that people walked into each other, into trees, into houses; wrecked cabs and touring cars, with all their lamps painted war blue lay along the roads and avenues. The Champs Elysées with its famous cafes and restaurants was as fearful as the Bois, yet lovers walked here still, cautiously, their arms about each other and on their arms the too familiar tin holding the too over-estimated gas mask, the mask that chokes you when even worn for a moment, and which looks like a portion of a deep-sea diving suit. I was told that it was *obligatoire;* if you appeared on the street without one, you were liable to arrest. I never had one, nor did I have the little pocket flashlight, one reason being that most of the time I was ill; the other was that when I got about to inquire, both were sold out.

Then the police regulations, the hours waiting in line to have your fingerprints taken and a *récépissé* granting a few days more. The long grotesque masses of frightened people, cut off from any communication with friends in other countries, or telephonic communication in their own, waiting to go through the legalities that might bring a receding world nearer, and always and everywhere that blue, the blue painted windows with their anti-splinter paper tapes. A giant painting from which the background and the purpose had been removed, that some unseen power might play his game of tic-tac-toe.

We have learned well or less well, how to live with the *décor* of custom, habit, and hope. Remove that suddenly and you have Paris. The childless gardens of the Luxembourg on whose lake tiny boats used to sail, under whose trees Punch hit Judy and children played ball, now left to the silent gray stone Queens, on whose outstretched hands pigeons stood motionless, as they must stand on Nelson's Monument in London. The parks turned earth up for the human mole that menaced man has become.

In each generation's flesh is the knowledge of a million generation's death. Still we do not get used to it, less endurable when it comes over nations all at once and men have to give up a personal death for a national death; to unwind the spool of his hoped-for destiny onto the bobbin of battle, this is called courage, but it is frightful. The women stand silently at deserted shop doors, or go about the streets saying little; the bells ring from the church towers as if they were unaware of the sandbags piled high about their base. Children huddled off to safety camps think it a lark and a holiday, and why is papa so silent and why does mother cry? Or if to cross the sea, why is everyone so gloomy about it? To cross the sea is a marvelous wonder; it will be fun to see a real submarine, exciting to get into lifeboats if a torpedo does sink the ship.

But having moved from hotel to hotel, as they were shut one after another, I knew how the women were taking it. The Athenia had gone down and the *couturieres* had smart Abri suits and snappy little bags to match for the gas mask that was so ugly.[1] Now there was hurry in the blood and zippers were on everything; chambermaids, who in most cases were obviously chambermaids of only a few days, wrung their hands above their aprons when you spoke to them kindly and asked for news. Shaking silently as dogs shake for something that is coming to pass a long way off, knowing the horror of its vibration without exact knowledge of its location. There was not one who had not someone at the front, brother, lover, husband. It was almost impossible to get a doctor, food was said to be guarded against hoarders, matches were giving out, and maids, left in charge of their mistresses' empty houses, stood without hope at the darkened windows.

Just before the first panic rush to the country, I got my third nurse, a monotonous-looking creature who refused to go to bed "because it is against the rules for a night nurse to sleep except sitting up." Her knitting needles clicked all night long like one of the monstrous women of the Revolution. She always answered any question with "the right thing is the right thing," for it hurt her to have to give ten percent of her wages to the nurses' agency, and she was trying to comfort herself by assuring herself and me that undoubtedly "the right thing *is* the right thing."

I do not know what it would be like to be well and in a war, possibly less terrifying than being ill, for ill one is doubly trapped, or one thinks so, which amounts to the same thing. Just at this time the rush for the country was in full tide. The American Embassy was called "the second weeping wall."

Americans crazy to get home and not at all dignified stormed the place, they crushed each other in shipping offices, the prices for reservations went up accordingly. I did not see this as I had no money to get back with, but I did participate in the run for the outlying districts. Almost the last person I knew who had not escaped was a young American boy, Johnny Coleman.[2] He phoned (one could still phone from private house to private house, and I was then with one of those maids I mentioned, whose mistress was away). He wanted to know did I wish to go with him and his father to Dangeau, on the little Loire. They had rented a house there up to the first of October. I did. Their car had broken down and there was no mechanic to be had; the engine was now running, but if it once stopped it would not start again. They would come for me, but I must make a dash and jump for it. On the way out we were only one of hundreds and hundreds of cars. Those going our way were piled high with mattresses, chairs, cooking pots and women sitting still and tense beside tense and still drivers. In the other direction, going toward Paris, were almost as many. We wondered why. It was soon too obvious: there were no women or children in that line, only young men, young men and some-times older men driving. They were going to war.

Coming into Dangeau, so small a town and seemingly so remote from trou-ble that we saw the Abri sign on nearly every house. People without any place to go were wandering across the fields, stopping at farms asking for hay and a place to sleep. Chartres was full of soldiers not even properly uniformed, some had blue caps on, all seemed at ease as people do who wander about a village green, but we knew that the windows of the cathedral were being removed and laid away in some crypt. The art treasures of Europe would be buried like Lazarus, to rise again in some distant time of peace.

The house was a little way out of the town, but all of us were nervous when a plane went overhead, and there seemed to be an incredible number of them. There was a Frenchman with us who had served in the last war. He said we were near a flying field. We said that this should be a protection. "Not at all," he said. "What goes up must come down, and if you shoot down an enemy plane and you get it, what? You also get back your shot." He spoke of the last war as "the ancient war," and sometimes he uneasily said "that baby war." At night we took as much precaution against our lights showing as we had in Paris. As the days passed, we got more and more nervous because, though possibly safer than in Paris, we were cut off from any communication at all. There was no telephone, there was no radio, and mails were late. The car, having come to a standstill, could not be got to move

[Page 8 missing; what follows is page 9.]

just a few miles from disaster.

One really does not know what to do with death. We may face it bravely or like cowards, but still we do not know what to do with it. I have been told by an army captain that no man ever went over the top without a jigger of rum or a dose of ether in his coffee. Is that a comment on bravery? Professors of psychoanalysis, or the newer doctors of the newer fad psychiatrics, might have something to say about man's maladjustment to death (of course, they could "cure" them of it, if prior to a war they had at least three years of warning, and if the soldiers had pockets full of money) just as they glibly talk about the maladjustment of man to his nerves. Certainly it is maladjustment, but why should a man be adjusted to horror, evil, war, and death? So, though none of us caught in Paris had seen one dead body, or heard many guns, or suffered any personal attack, neither imprisonment nor loss of men, still the fear was there, and the nerves giving way.

The story closes on my last nurse and my return to America. The young boy sailed for America, and I returned to my hotel. There was no one to talk to, no friend left, and the only one I cared for was in Aix-en-Provence.[3] My other friends were in London. Again my nerves broke, but I had to stand in line hour upon hour for the permission to stay in France. When I inquired if the Comité Americain de Secours Civil could use me, I was laughed at. Americans were not wanted in France, and why on earth was I still there after nearly seven weeks? I said it was a very simple matter—I had no money.

I took a taxi and instantly that taxi was rammed in the back by another, throwing me against the front glass, my nose and lip cut and bleeding, but that did not prevent the driver from using the divine privilege of French chauffeurs. He arose from his seat, twirling his thumbs in his ears, to me an obscure insult, cursing in argot dating from the time of Rabelais, if not earlier. I pled with him to stop and to take me home. I had been in bed not longer than an hour when the hotel caught fire. The *garçon* very cheerfully said it was only the cave. I went back to bed, choking with the smoke.

It must have been about eleven or eleven thirty when I was wakened with the screaming of the sirens. I heard the hotel emptying, feet running along the corridors and down the steps, and that sound, which I had never heard before, is a very unnerving thing.

I opened my door and watched them go. Some were powdering their noses, and some painting their lips, some wore the smart sweater and slacks known as Abri wear, and all carried the inevitable gas mask that I knew was not good for anything, unless a high official who had told me so was lying. "They are just to keep the people from panic." I went back to bed and waited until I heard them all coming back again, laughing and talking as people do who have just gone through a bad moment.

So I got my last nurse. I was shaking and could not stop it. What would I have been like had I been in Poland? She was a prize; I really believe she had graduated as nurse straight from Les Halles. She was all hoof, she was half blind (at the highest point in my fever I had to watch her, for she has a passion for getting the medicines mixed), and she could not hear, or rather she had no time for hearing, as she never stopped talking from the time she arrived to the time that she left. Like all the other nurses, she assured me that she had never sunk so low before; she had never been on duty in anything less grand than the Ritz and had almost never nursed below the grade of princess or baron. She talked with the high, screaming velocity common to a certain type of Parisienne. She was proud of that voice, of its shattering effects. Yet she was never there when I wanted her. I discovered why: she was doing her laundry and her husband's pants in my bathtub.

On the 24th of October, 1939, I was pushed on a train by Peggy Guggenheim, a pillow thrown at me straight in my face from the platform. You could not buy passage on a ship except in dollars, and she had the dollars, so I won't attempt to describe that night in the train, the widow in black, arms down on my chest, the landing the next morning in Bordeaux, the lack of porters, and the day and night to live through before the train to Verdon. Then the hours of red tape before you were allowed on board, the discovery that the ship was so packed that six to a cabin was comparatively comfortable to the condition of some, who were twenty to a room (the nursery). One of the six was an old lady with a broken arm who was very brave, but would talk; another had curvature of the spine and was brave about that too; a third was a seasick little bride who had had to leave her French husband in France, and who cried between groans, "Where is that steward? I can't, I positively can't go across the sea without my collapsible slippers." And everyone waiting for that shock which would mean death at sea. It was night when the Statue of Liberty, all aglow, came into sight seeming to move around the ship as we swung into harbor.

Where no one knows what Europe is really like (just as the European does not know what America is like), opulent (in spite of the twelve to thirteen million out of work) with ice-cream sodas, frigidaires, pretty clothes, handsome homes, and safety. But what is wrong even here? One is in a city that should be a little less nervous than Paris or a London, and yet as so many are breaking down, taking to health cures, Science, Christian or otherwise.[4]

The Helping Brotherhood, and that newest of helps for the rich and jittery, psychiatry. Sanatoriums are full, and Father Divine shaking the blood of the blacks. Why?

Back in Paris are a man or two, a woman or two of my own race, who have said that they would run like mad if there was a war, but they are playing cards.[5]

Notes
Bibliography

Notes

Introduction

I. James Scott's unpublished interview with DB, 2 April 1971, in Herring, *Djuna*, 175.

2. The University of Delaware has the Emily Holmes Coleman Archive, which contains all of Barnes's letters to Coleman, who helped edit *Nightwood* and first approached T. S. Eliot about publishing this novel. The Barnes–Coleman correspondence is the single most important collection of letters related to Barnes and the most revealing. A selection of the letters has recently been published in German, without the original English, by Mary Lynn Broe (*Im Dunkeln gehen: Briefe an Emily Coleman*). See also Herring, *Djuna*, and Cheryl J. Plumb's introduction to her scholarly annotated edition of *Nightwood*.

3. O'Neal in Broe, *Silence and Power*, 360.

4. See Herring and Stutman, "Djuna Barnes: Eighteen Poems."

5. In 1962 Farrar, Straus, and Cudahy published the *Selected Works of Djuna Barnes*, a work that reprinted certain of her stories, her play *The Antiphon*, and *Nightwood*, but omitted all her poems.

6. This comment appears on a page of notes in series III, box 7 that begins with the phrase "Undoubtedly the reason why uniforms . . ."

7. Emily Coleman to DB, 27 August 1935, 7.

8. Mary Pyne acted in Provincetown Players productions. DB was in love with her for several years. Ernst "Putzi" Hanfstaengl (1887–1975) was Hitler's minister for the foreign press in the 1930s; prior to World War I, he was engaged to DB. He wrote *Unheard Witness* (1967) and *Zwischen Weissem und Braunem Haus* (1970).

9. DB to Emily Coleman, 21 May 1938 (University of Delaware).

10. See Herring, *Djuna*, 276, 345.

11. This note is on a page in series III, box 7, folder 6.

12. For an account of DB's friendship with Joyce and her interview with him, see Herring, "Djuna Barnes Remembers James Joyce."

13. In series III, box 7, folder 3. On another page she remembered the anonymous comment as "The day of Failure" (series III, box 7, folder 6). Apparently Joyce was so nervous because *Ulysses* was published on this day.

14. See Antheil's *Bad Boy of Music*, 184, where he says, "The 'Ballet Mécanique' is really

scored for eight grand pianos, to say nothing of xylophones, percussion, and what not." Perhaps the concert that DB was thinking of is described by Antheil on 7–8.

15. Broe, *Silence and Power*, 356.

16. Levine, "Works in Progress," 187.

17. Tyler-Bennett, "'Thick Within Our Hair.'"

18. Interview with Hank O'Neal, New York, January 1992.

19. See Herring, *Djuna*, 249.

20. Eliot, *Selected Essays*, 241.

21. John Hayward (1905–65) was a poet, scholar, essayist, and former apartment mate of T. S. Eliot. Scholars may wish to consider the relationship of Barnes's evolving poetic form to the volumes of literary criticism that she owned. In addition to many of Eliot's, the list includes William Wimsatt's *Verbal Icon*, R. P. Blackmur's *Form and Value in Modern Poetry*, John Crowe Ransom's *World's Body*, Allen Tate's *Hovering Fly*, and William Empson's *Seven Types of Ambiguity*.

22. Broe, *Silence and Power*, 359.

23. Ibid., 360.

24. Herring, *Djuna*, 254.

25. Ibid., 289. Letter from DB to Emily Coleman, 22 October 1965.

26. Barnes owned two works by Emile Male (1862–1954), *Religious Art from the Twelfth to the Eighteenth Century* and *The Gothic Image: Religious Art in France of the Thirteenth Century.*

27. Hank O'Neal published *"Life is painful, nasty and short . . . in my case it has only been painful and nasty": An Informal Memoir of Djuna Barnes.*

28. Giles, *History of Chinese Literature*, 100. The editors' source is Wai-lim Yip, *Ezra Pound's Cathay*, 64.

29. Pound, *The Lustra of Ezra Pound, with the Earlier Poems.*

30. Giles, *History of Chinese Literature*, 100.

Notes toward the Memoirs

1. Readers interested in DB's memories of her Paris years should also read her *Vagaries Malicieux*. Here she elaborates on her impressions of James Joyce, whom she had previously interviewed.

2. Herring, *Djuna*, 246–48.

Selected Notes on T. S. Eliot

1. John Hayward and Eliot were apartment mates. See note 21 in the introduction.

2. At the top of this page is the date 1981.

3. Janet Flanner (1892–1978) was the Paris correspondent for the *New Yorker*.

4. Eliot often stayed with the publisher Robert Giroux (1914–) when in New York. Giroux published DB's *Selected Works* in 1962.

5. *The Sacred Wood* (1920) was Eliot's first volume of literary criticism.

6. Peter du Sautoy (1893–1992) was T. S. Eliot's colleague at Faber & Faber.

7. T. S. Eliot's play *The Elder Statesman* was published in 1958.

8. Frank Morley was a friend and colleague of Eliot's at Faber & Faber.

9. Stevie Smith, pen name of Florence Margaret Smith (1902–71), British poet and novelist. T. S. Eliot's play *The Family Reunion* was published in 1959; DB's *Antiphon* in 1961.

10. Edwin Muir (1887–1959), Scottish poet, and friend of both DB and Eliot. Dag Hammarskjöld (1905–61), Swedish statesman, former secretary general of the United Nations, and friend of DB. He helped translate *The Antiphon* into Swedish. The play premiered in Stockholm in 1961.

11. Paul Tillich (1886–1965) published his *Systematic Theology* (3 vols.) between 1951 and 1963.

12. Laurence Vail (1891–1968), French-born American writer and friend of DB.

13. These notes toward the memoirs are typed, but DB occasionally inserted notes in cursive.

14. Apparently DB has forgotten the precise word—thus the space and question mark.

15. A collection of James Joyce's manuscripts was exhibited in the Institute of Contemporary Arts, Dover Street, London, in June 1950. The collection was eventually purchased by the University of Buffalo (now SUNY at Buffalo).

16. Valerie Fletcher, later Mrs. T. S. Eliot, was Eliot's secretary at the publishers Faber & Faber.

17. Max Beerbohm (1872–1956), English essayist and caricaturist; H. G. Wells (1866–1946), English novelist and journalist.

18. Thomas Middleton (1580–1627), English dramatist. "The Roaring Girl" was written with Thomas Dekker.

Vantage Ground

1. Gertrude Stein (1874–1946), American author of *Three Lives* (1909) and *Tender Buttons* (1914).

2. Ernest Hemingway (1898–1961) published *For Whom the Bell Tolls* in 1940.

3. Leo Stein (1872–1947), American art critic.

4. Fernand Crommelynck (1886–1970) published his play *Le Cocu Magnifique* in 1921. Jean Cocteau (1889–1963), French poet, novelist, dramatist, essayist, film writer, and director.

5. *Le Boeuf sur le Toit* (1920), by Cocteau, was a modernistic ballet with music by Darius Milhaud and décor by Raoul Dufy. The play lent its name to this cabaret.

6. These writers were associated with the Parisian avant-guard: Tristan Tzara (1896–1963), Romanian poet; Philippe Soupault (1897–1990), French poet, novelist, and critic; Paul Éluard (1895–1952), pen name of Eugene Grindel, French poet; Jacques Baron (1905–), French author; Robert Desnos (1900–45), French poet involved with surrealism (see DB *Interviews*, 298); Louis Aragon (1897–1982), French novelist, poet, essayist, also involved with surrealism.

7. A narrative about Cocteau is deleted here, in favor of a more complete draft in the pages to come.

8. Gabrielle "Coco" Bonheur Chanel (1883–1971), fashion designer. DB's interview with Chanel appeared in September 1931. DB, *Interviews*, 376–82.

9. The Fratellini brothers (Francois, Paul, Albert) were clowns at the Cirque d'Hiver.

10. Cocteau's theatrical production of *Orphée* opened in 1926.

11. Georges Pitoëff (1886–1939) and his wife were actors.

12. The identity of James Lover is unknown.

13. Cocteau's novel *Les enfants terribles* appeared in 1929.

14. Comte Étienne de Beaumont was a socialite and a promoter of cultural events. Cocteau produced ballets for Diaghilev's Ballet Russe. Pound refers to Ezra Pound (1885–1972), the American poet and critic. George Antheil (1900–58) was an American avant-garde composer. The bracketed phrase was moved from a later repetitious description of this concert.

15. Paul Poiret, a fashion designer in Paris, was among the first to create art deco. Mentioned in DB, *Interviews*, 300.

16. Sylvia Beach (1887–1962), publisher of James Joyce's *Ulysses* (1922). The word "summoner" was written "Sumner."

17. DB wrote "dialogue" but clearly meant "monologue."

18. James Joyce (1882–1941) was mistakenly christened James Augusta Joyce. To avoid repetition, the bracketed insertion has been transferred from a later section.

19. Charles Stewart Parnell (1846–91) was an Irish nationalist leader in Parliament and to Joyce a martyr.

20. Ford Madox Ford (1873–1939) founded the *transatlantic review* in Paris in 1922. Peter Neagoe (1881–1963), Romanian-American writer and coeditor of *New Review*, was DB's lover in the 1930s.

21. James Joyce's *Finnegans Wake* was published in 1939, *A Portrait of the Artist as a Young Man* in 1916.

22. James Joyce's *Pomes Penyeach* was published in 1927. A repetitive phrase in the sentence has been transferred elsewhere.

23. Le Bal des Quartres Arts (Four Arts Ball) was a costume party by students at the École des Beaux-Arts often held in the Salle Wagram.

24. In 1930 the Marquis Boni de Castellane rented the entire Bois de Boulogne for a party. In a later section of this narrative, DB suggests that his source of income was an American heiress, Anna Gould. DB mentions them in her *Interviews*, 321.

25. T. S. Eliot's play *Murder in the Cathedral* was published in 1935.

26. The reference is unclear: perhaps Charles Ives (1874–1954), American composer; David Teniers the Elder (1582–1649), painter; David Teniers the Younger (1610–90), painter; Giovanni Colonna (1637–95), Italian composer, organist, and choirmaster.

27. Victor Hugo (1802–83), French writer.

28. Toulouse-Lautrec (1864–1901) often drew Yvette Guilbert (1867–1944), a singer interviewed by DB in 1917 (*Interviews*, 263–71).

29. DB's grandmother Zadel Barnes (1841–1917) mentioned this story to DB. Cetshwayo (Cetewayo) was the last great Zulu king (1826?–1884). Another note by DB (series III, box 7, folder 7) reads: "Catewayo who gave my grandmother a mooyum car (only know the sound of the word), a flat fish-like piece of wood (carved ends), which swung around the head on a cord, gave a moaning sound. Was it the deposed king of the Zulus, a black who was subsequently restored to a portion of his kingdom?"

30. Aeschylus (525–456 BC), Greek dramatist.

31. Isadora Duncan (1878–1927), American dancer.

32. Allen Tate (1899–1979), poet, critic, novelist, teacher, and friend of DB.

33. Marcel Duchamp (1887–1968), French painter, Dadaist, and friend of DB.

34. DB's grandmother Zadel wrote love letters of a sexual nature to the young DB, which she saved. DB arrived at the family's Long Island farm about two hours before Zadel's death on 16 May 1917. One can well imagine her destitute father asking for burial money since the body was to be transported for burial to Middletown, Connecticut.

35. There were several painters with the surname Milanese, but the reference could also be to residents of Milan.

36. Les Vikings was a café, restaurant, and hotel in the rue Vavin.

37. DB later mentions Flossie Martin as a singer who lost her voice on gin. She acted in the film *Galérie des monstres* in 1923 (Tyler-Bennett, "Thick Within Our Hair," 107). Joe Zelli owned a nightclub in Pigalle, Au Zelli's. The next lines mention other nightclubs in Paris.

38. Lady Duff Twysden (1893–1938), born Mary Duff Byrom, married Sir Roger William Twysden, tenth Baronet (1894–1934). She is mentioned in DB, *Interviews*, 334.

39. Here the narrative ends. Mimi Franchetti was part of the Natalie Barney circle, caricatured as "Senorita Flyabout" in DB's *Ladies Almanack* (1928). Compton MacKenzie (1883–1972) published *Extraordinary Women* in 1928.

A Way of Life

1. DB interviewed the Principesa San Faustino (Jane Campbell) in Rome in 1927. See DB, *Interviews*, 315–24.

2. Etienne Balsan is mentioned in DB, *Interviews*, 376–77.

3. Armand, Comte de la Rochfoucauld; Henri, Marquis de la Falaise de la Coudraie, husband of Gloria Swanson.

4. Comte Robert de Montesquiou (1855–1921), friend of Natalie Barney.

5. Repetitive material following the phrase "who spoke better Italian than English or French" has been deleted. Here and elsewhere in this narrative, repetitive material indicated by bracketed ellipses has either been transferred elsewhere or deleted.

6. Frank Budgen (1882–1971), author of *James Joyce and the Making of Ulysses.* A repetitive phrase following Budgen's name has been deleted.

7. Deleted here is a repetitive memoir of Les Halles and Black Velvet.

8. Edna St. Vincent Millay (1892–1950), American poet, married Eugen Jan Boissevain in 1923.

9. Sinclair Lewis (1885–1951) published *Dodsworth* in 1929.

10. Dorothy Thompson (1893–1961), American author.

11. A short, repetitive memoir of Marie Laurencin following this sentence is omitted.

12. Kay Boyle (1902–92), American writer of whom DB was not fond.

13. Robert McAlmon (1896–1956), perhaps best known for *Being Geniuses Together* (1938).

14. Edmund Wilson (1895–1972), American writer and critic. He and DB were not fond of each other. Edith Wharton (1862–1937) published *Ethan Frome* in 1911. Wilson liked the novel, but DB didn't.

15. Perhaps this is the American writer Albert J. Nock (1872–1945).

16. The Gurdjieff reference is to Georges Gurdjieff (1872–1949), hypnotherapist. Margaret Anderson wrote a book about him.

17. Raymond Radiguet (1903–23), protégé of Cocteau, died of typhoid fever.

18. Princess Lucien Murat, Comtesse de Chambrun (1876–1951), mentioned in DB, *Interviews*, 301. Jacques Baron, André Breton, Philippe Soupault, Tristan Tzara, Robert Desnos, Paul Éluard, and Pierre de Massot were surrealist poets, all French except Tzara, who was Romanian.

19. Arthur Waley (1889–1966), English Orientalist. His most important works include his translations of Chinese poetry and of the Japanese novel *The Tale of Genji* (1925–33) by Murasaki Shikibu. Among his other works are *The No Plays of Japan* (1921), *The Poetry and Career of Li Po* (1959), and *The Secret History of the Mongols and Other Pieces* (1964). More importantly for Barnes studies, he published *A Hundred and Seventy Chinese Poems* (1918), which Barnes must have read for her poem "To the Dead Favourite of Liu Ch'e."

Jean de Bosschaire (1878–1953), Belgian novelist, poet, painter, and illustrator; Isidore Ducasse, Comte de Lautreamont (1846–70), revered by the surrealists; Jean Giraudoux (1882–1944), French novelist, dramatist, critic; Rainer Maria Rilke (1875–1926), poet and novelist born in Prague, he wrote in German.

20. A second reference to Le Boeuf sur le Toit was deleted here.

Farewell Paris

1. Hilaire Hiler (i.e., Hiler Hartzberg) (1898–1966), painter and decorator. Lynn Holcomb (1903–48) was a newspaperman and editor in Ohio.

2. Père Lachaise Cemetery in Paris.

3. Daniel Mahoney (late 1880s–1959), Left Bank character and the model for Dr. Matthew O'Connor in DB's novel *Nightwood*. Curie is probably Madame Eve Curie (1867–1934), who was director of research at the Radium Institute (1918–34).

4. Marie Laurencin (1883–1956), painter, mistress of Apollinaire, mentioned in DB, *Interviews*, 301. Another fragment clarifies this note; it is in series III, box 8, folder 2 of the UMD Barnes Collection. Barnes mentions that Laurencin had a lover who was "terrified at the mere sight of firearms. So Laurencin always carried a small arm in her hand-bag that (she said) he might sense it when she looked at him. One day she took a *bateau mouche* to the Louvre to meet another man. It was July 14. And who was in the boat? Her lover. He said 'Where are you going?' She replied, 'To the Louvre.' He said, 'Why do you tell me that? You know the Louvre is closed on the 14th of July.' She said, 'It will open for me.'"

5. Radiguet's *Le Diable au corps* was published in 1923. A repetitive phrase has been eliminated at the end of the sentence.

6. A repetitive phrase has been transferred to another place in the narrative.

7. The phrase "the strongest concoction known to man" was brought here from a deleted similar narrative on Joyce in "Vantage Ground."

8. "I am a priest."

9. A repetitive phrase in the sentence has been deleted.

10. Margaret C. Anderson (1886–1973) and Jane Heap (1883–1964) were editors of the *Little Review*. Joyce's benefactor was Harriet Weaver (1876–1961).

11. Mary Butts (1890–1937), British writer, lived with Cecil Maitland (d. 1927).

12. Francis Picabia (1879–1953), French avant-garde artist.

13. Marsden Hartley (1877–1943); Charles Demuth (1883–1935).

14. Glenway Westcott (1901–87), American writer. The Courbet allusion is probably to Gustave Courbet (1819–77), French painter.

15. Constantin Brancusi (1876–1957), Romanian sculptor and longtime Parisian.

16. Harold Stearns (1891–1943), American writer.

17. Mary Louise Reynolds (1891–1950) lived with Marcel Duchamp. Her papers and books are at the Art Institute of Chicago.

18. Baroness Elsa von Freytag Loringhoven (1874–1927), German-American collage artist and close friend of DB.

19. The Slavinsky DB mentions may be the Russian writer Evgenii Slavinsky (1898–1978).

20. Allan Ross MacDougall and Irma Duncan, *Isadora Duncan's Russian Days and Her Last Days in France* (1929). Allan Ross MacDougall, *The Gourmets Almanac, wherein is set down, month by month, recipes for strange and exotic dishes, with divers considerations . . .* (1931).

21. Natalie Clifford Barney (1876–1972), American writer and lesbian socialite.

22. Rémy de Gourmont (1858–1915), French critic and essayist, friend of Barney.

23. Only selected names will be identified: Anatole France (1844–1924), French novelist, poet, and critic; Pierre Louys (1870–1925), French novelist and poet; Daniel Berthelot (1865–1927), French writer; Guillaume Apollinaire (1880–1918), poet, novelist, and dramatist; Israel Zangwill (1864–1926), British writer, born in London of Russian-Jewish parents; Georg Brandes (1842–1927), Danish literary critic and scholar; Colette (1873–1954), pen name of Sidonie Gabrielle Colette, French novelist; Carl Van Vechten (1880–1964), American critic and novelist; Max Jacob (1876–1944) French writer and painter; Mary Lilian, Lady Rothermere (died 1937), wife of Harold Harmsworth, the first Vicount Rothermere (1868–1940), who, with his brother Alfred, published the *Daily Mail* and other newspapers (she financed the magazine *Criterion* when T. S. Eliot was editor); Richard Le Gallienne (1867–1947), British writer; Eva Le Gallienne (1899–1991), actress; Elisabeth de Gramont, duchesse de Clermont-Tonnerre (1875–1954), French writer mentioned in Flanner, *Paris Was Yesterday*, 43–44, and also DB, *Interviews*, 323 (DB owned her book *Robert de Montesquiou et Marcel Proust* (1925); Rachilde (1860–1953), French writer; Edouard Herriot (1872–1957), French statesman; Arthur Symonds (1865–1945), perhaps best known for *The Symbolist Movement in Literature* (1899); André Germain (1881–), French critic.

24. Lucie Delarue Mardrus (1875–1945), French writer; Mina Loy (1882–1966), British poet, painter, friend of DB.

25. Sara Bernhardt (1844–1923), French actress, the best-known stage figure of her time.

26. Charles Lindberg (1902–74), American aviator.

27. For Edouard Herriot, see note 23.

28. Konrad Bercovici (1882–1961), Romanian-American writer, friend of DB.

29. Frank Harris (1856–1931). His *My Life and Loves* (3 vols.) appeared 1923–27.

30. (Edward) Aleister Crowley (1875–1947), English poet and author of books on magic and occult lore.

31. Katherine Mansfield (1888–1923), New Zealand-born short-story writer and poet.

32. Robert Winthrop Chanler (1872?–1930), American painter.

33. Jules Pascin (1885–1930), Bulgarian-born French painter.

34. Hermine David (1886–1971).

35. Louise Bryant (1885–1936), partner of John "Jack" Reed (1887–1920), American journalist buried in the Kremlin. Bryant was the author of *Six Red Months in Russia* (1918). William Christian Bullitt (1891–1967), American ambassador to Russia, 1933–36. They are discussed in Antheil, *Bad Boy of Music*, 175, 270.

36. Black Velvet is stout and champagne. "Sculptress" has been transferred here from a deleted repetition elsewhere.

37. DB interviewed Kiki de Montparnasse (Alice Prin) in 1924. See DB, *Interviews*, 297–303. Man Ray (1890–1977), American painter, photographer, and filmmaker.

38. Anna Wickham (1884–1947), English writer.

39. The Wildenstein Gallery was in New York. Sir Gerald Kelly (1879–1972) was a portrait, figure, and landscape painter.

40. Unidentified.

41. The next sentence is repetitive and has been deleted.

42. This bracketed text is from another draft of DB's Antheil memoir.

43. Edward W. Titus (1870–1952) owned a bookshop in Paris, the Black Manikin, in the rue Delambre. When DB's *Ladies Almanack* was published, Titus tried unethical tactics to profit from the sale of the book. See Herring, *Djuna*, 152–53.

44. James Light (1894–1964) was actor and director for the Provincetown Players.

45. Berenice Abbott (1898–1991), American photographer and friend of DB.

46. William Bird (1888–1963), journalist, printer, founder of the Three Mountain Press in Paris. He helped with the printing of DB's *Ladies Almanack*.

47. Gene Tunney (1897–1978), American boxer; Alex Small (1895–1965), journalist for the *Chicago Tribune*.

48. Thornton Wilder's (1897–1975). *The Bridge of San Luis Rey* (1927) won the Pulitzer Prize.

49. (Ferdinand-Victor) Eugene Delacroix (1798–1863), French painter; Victor Hugo (1802–85), French writer.

50. Michael Romanoff (1890–1971), born Harry Gerguson. This impostor showed up in Paris in 1919 claiming to be a Russian prince, son of Alexander III. Eventually he opened a successful restaurant in Beverly Hills, California, where he was popular with patrons from the film industry who enjoyed being duped. There is a fascinating obituary in the *New York Times* for 3 September 1971.

51. Moise Kisling (1891–1953), artist and critic in Paris, is mentioned in DB, *Interviews*, 298. A repetitive phrase has been deleted from this sentence; the following repetitive sentence has also been deleted.

War in Paris (1939)

1. *Abri* is the French word for "shelter," but in this case it is a line of clothing.

2. John Coleman was the son of DB's friend Emily Holmes Coleman.

3. This is probably DB's former lover Thelma Wood (1901–70), the Robin of *Nightwood*.

4. During DB's absence from New York, her mother had become a fervent convert to Christian Science. Because she had neither job nor money, DB had to live with her, and they did not get along. Soon her family would put her into a sanatorium to dry out.

5. At the bottom of the last page of one copy of "War in Paris" is the note: "All awful—saved for reference."

Bibliography

Selected Works of Djuna Barnes

The Book of Repulsive Women. Bruno Chap Books 2, no. 6 (13 November 1915): 86–112. (Contains "From Fifth Avenue Up," "In General," "From Third Avenue On," "Seen from the 'L,'" "In Particular," "Twilight of the Illicit," "To a Cabaret Dancer," "Suicide," and five drawings.) Reprint, Los Angeles: Sun and Moon Press, 1994.

A Book. New York: Boni & Liveright, 1923.

Ladies Almanack (Written by a lady of fashion). Dijon, France: Darantière (privately printed), 1928. Reprints, New York: Harper & Row, 1972; Elmwood Park, Ill.: Dalkey Archive Press, 1992.

Ryder. New York: Boni & Liveright, 1928. Reprints, St. Martin's Press, 1979, 1981; Elmwood Park, Ill.: Dalkey Archive Press, 1990.

A Night Among the Horses. New York: Boni & Liveright, 1929. (A new edition of *A Book* with three stories added.)

Nightwood. London: Faber & Faber, 1936. Reprints, New York: Harcourt, Brace, 1937; Cambridge, Mass.: Ryerson Press, 1936; New York: New Directions, 1946; London: Faber & Faber, 1950; New York: Farrar, Straus & Cudahy, 1962 (in *Selected Works*).

Nightwood: The Original Version and Related Drafts. Edited by Cheryl J. Plumb. Normal, Ill.: Dalkey Archive Press, 1995.

The Antiphon. London: Faber & Faber; New York: Farrar, Straus & Cudahy, 1958. Reprint, New York: Farrar, Straus & Cudahy, 1962 (in *Selected Works*); Los Angeles: Green Integer, 2000.

Spillway. London: Faber & Faber. Reprints, New York: Farrar, Straus & Cudahy, 1962 (in *Selected Works*); New York: Harper & Row, 1972.

Vagaries Malicieux. New York: F. Hallman, 1974. Originally published in *The Double Dealer*, May 1922, 249–60 (On Paris).

Greenwich Village as It Is. Edited by Robert A. Wilson. New York: Phoenix Book Shop, 1978 (in *New York*).

Selected Works of Djuna Barnes (*Spillway, The Antiphon, Nightwood*). New York: Farrar, Straus & Cudahy, 1962. Reprint, 1980.

Creatures in an Alphabet. New York: Dial Press, 1982.

Smoke and Other Early Stories. Edited by Douglas Messerli. College Park, Md.: Sun & Moon Press, 1982. 2nd ed., 1987.

Interviews. Edited by Alyce Barry. Washington, D.C.: Sun & Moon Press, 1985.

New York. Edited by Alyce Barry. Los Angeles: Sun & Moon Press, 1989.

Collected Stories. Edited by Phillip Herring. Los Angeles: Sun & Moon Press, 1996.

Poe's Mother: Selected Drawings of Djuna Barnes. Edited by Douglas Messerli. Los Angeles: Sun & Moon Press, 1996.

Poesía Reunida, 1911–1982. Texts in English and Spanish. Selected, edited, and translated by Osías Stutman. Montblanc (Tarragona), Spain: Igitur/Poesía, 2004.

Works Cited and Consulted

Allen, Carolyn. "Djuna Barnes: Looking Like a (Lesbian) Poet." In *The Modern Woman Revisited: Paris between the Wars,* edited by Whitney Chadwick and Tirza True Latimer, 145–54. New Brunswick, N.J.: Rutgers University Press, 2003.

Antheil, George. *Bad Boy of Music.* Garden City, N.Y.: Doubleday, Doran, 1945.

Barnes, Djuna. "Aller et Retour." *transatlantic review,* April 1924, 159–67.

Blackmur, R. P. *Form and Value in Modern Poetry.* Garden City, N.Y.: Doubleday Anchor Books, 1957.

Braithwaite, W. S., ed. *Anthology of Magazine Verse for 1918 and Year Book of American Poetry.* Boston: Small, Maynard, 1918.

Braybrooke, Neville, ed. *T. S. Eliot: A Symposium for His Seventieth Birthday.* New York: Farrar, Straus & Cudahy, New York, 1958.

———, ed. *The Wind and the Rain: An Easter Book for 1962.* London: Secker & Warburg, 1962.

Broe, Mary Lynn. *Im Dunkeln gehen: Briefe an Emily Coleman.* Berlin: Wagenbach, 2002.

———. *Silence and Power: A Reevaluation of Djuna Barnes.* Carbondale: Southern Illinois University Press, 1991.

Burton, Robert. *The Anatomy of Melancholy.* 1621. Reprint, New York: AMS Press, 1973.

Campo, Cristina, trans. *Conoscenza Religiosa,* January–March, 1969, 69–70.

Caselli, Daniela. "'Elementary, My Dear Djuna': Unreadable Simplicity in Barnes' *Creatures in an Alphabet.*" *Critical Survey* 13, no. 3 (2001): 89–112.

Clermont-Tonnerre, Elisabeth de. *Robert de Montesquiou et Marcel Proust.* Paris: Flammarion, 1925.

Donne, John. *The Complete Poetry and Selected Prose.* Edited by C. M. Coffin. New York: Modern Library, 1952.

Eliot, T. S. *The Elder Statesman.* London: Faber, 1959.

———. *The Sacred Wood.* London: Methuen, 1920.

———. *Selected Essays, 1919–32.* New York: Harcourt, Brace, 1932.

Empson, William. *Seven Types of Ambiguity.* New York: Meridian, 1955.

Faulkner, William. *Intruder in the Dust.* 1948. Reprint, New York: Vintage Books, 1991.

Field, Andrew. *Djuna: The Life and Times of Djuna Barnes.* New York: G. P. Putnam & Sons, 1983.

Flanner, Janet. *Paris Was Yesterday: 1925–1939.* New York: Popular Library, 1970.

Fuchs, Miriam. "Djuna Barnes and T. S. Eliot: Authority, Resistance, and Acquiescence." *Tulsa Studies in Women's Literature* 12 (Fall 1993): 289–313.

Galvin, Mary E. *Queer Poetics: Five Modernist Women Writers.* Westport, Conn.: Praetor, 1999.

Germain, E. B., ed. *Surrealist Poetry in English.* London: Penguin Books, 1978.

Giles, Herbert Allen. *A History of Chinese Literature.* New York: D. Appleton, 1901.

Glidzen, A., ed. *A Festschrift for Djuna Barnes on Her 80th Birthday.* Kent, Ohio: Kent State University Press, 1972.

Grierson, Herbert. *Metaphysical Lyrics and Poems of the Seventeenth Century.* Oxford: Oxford University Press, 1921.

Hall, James. *Dictionary of Subjects and Symbols in Art.* New York: Harper & Row, Icon Editions, 1979.

Hayward, John, ed. *Seventeenth Century Poetry: An Anthology.* London: Chatto & Windus, 1948.

Herring, Phillip. "Djuna Barnes Remembers James Joyce." *James Joyce Quarterly* 30 (Fall 1992): 113–17.

———. *Djuna: The Life and Work of Djuna Barnes.* New York: Viking Press, 1995.

Herring, Phillip, and Osías Stutman. "Djuna Barnes: Eighteen Poems." *Conjunctions* 31 (1998): 73–80.

Levine, Nancy L. "Works in Progress: The Uncollected Poetry of Barnes' Patchin Place Period." *The Review of Contemporary Fiction* 13, no. 3 (Fall 1993): 187–200.

Loncraine, Rebecca, ed. *Djuna Barnes: The Book of Repulsive Women and Other Poems.* London: Routledge, 2003.

———. "The Book of Repulsive Women: Djuna Barnes' Unknown Poetry." *PN Review* 29, no. 6 (July–August 2003): 40–45.

Male, Émile. *The Gothic Image: Religious Art in France of the Thirteenth Century.* New York: Harper & Row, 1972.

———. *Religious Art from the Twelfth to the Eighteenth Century.* New York: Noonday Books, 1958.

Massingham, H. J., ed. *A Treasury of Seventeenth Century English Verse from the Death of Shakespeare to the Restoration (1616–1660).* London: Macmillan, 1931.

O'Neal, Hank. *"Life is painful, nasty and short . . . in my case it has only been painful and nasty": An Informal Memoir of Djuna Barnes.* New York: Paragon 1990.

Pound, Ezra. *Collected Shorter Poems.* London: Faber & Faber, 1952.

———. *The Lustra of Ezra Pound, with the Earlier Poems.* New York: Knopf, 1917.

———. *The Cantos of Ezra Pound.* New York: New Directions, 1986.

Ransom, John Crowe. *The World's Body.* New York: Charles Scribner's Sons, 1938.

Ruthven, K. K. *A Guide to Ezra Pound's Personae.* 1926. Reprint, Berkeley: University of California Press, 1969.

Santayana, George. *Three Philosophical Poets.* Cambridge, Mass.: Harvard University Press, 1910.

Schuchard, Ronald, ed. *T. S. Eliot: The Varieties of Metaphysical Poetry.* London: Faber & Faber, 1993. Reprint, New York: Harvest Books, 1996.

Tate, Allen. *The Hovering Fly and Other Essays.* Cummington, Mass.: Cummington Press, 1949.

Tillich, Paul. *Systematic Theology.* 3 vols. Chicago: University of Chicago Press, 1951–63.

Tyler-Bennett, Deborah. "'Thick Within Our Hair': Djuna Barnes' Gothic Lovers." In *Gothic Modernisms,* edited by Andrew Smith and Jeff Wallace, 95–110. New York: Palgrave Publishers, 2001.

Waley, Arthur, trans. *A Hundred and Seventy Chinese Poems.* New York: Knopf, 1919.

Wimsatt, William, Jr. *The Verbal Icon: Studies in the Meaning of Poetry.* New York: Noonday, 1958.

Yip, Wai-lim. *Ezra Pound's Cathay.* Princeton, N.J.: Princeton University Press, 1969.